Debating History

DEBATES ON THE SOVIET UNION'S COLLAPSE

John Allen

ReferencePoint Press®

San Diego, CA

About the Author
John Allen is a writer living in Oklahoma City.

© 2019 ReferencePoint Press, Inc.
Printed in the United States

For more information, contact:
ReferencePoint Press, Inc.
PO Box 27779
San Diego, CA 92198
www.ReferencePointPress.com

LIBRARY OF CONGRESS CATALOGING-IN-PUBLICATION DATA

Names: Allen, John, 1957– author.
Title: Debates on the Soviet Union's Collapse/by John Allen.
Description: San Diego, CA: ReferencePoint Press, Inc., [2019] | Series:
   Debating History series | Includes bibliographical references and index. |
   Audience: Grades 9–12.
Identifiers: LCCN 2017054542 (print) | LCCN 2018015906 (ebook) | ISBN
   9781682823767 (eBook) | ISBN 9781682823750 (hardback)
Subjects: LCSH: Soviet Union—History—Juvenile literature. | Soviet
   Union—Military policy—Juvenile literature. |
   Afghanistan—History—Soviet occupation, 1979–1989—Juvenile literature. |
   Gorbachev, Mikhail Sergeevich, 1931—Juvenile literature. | Russia
   (Federation)—Foreign relations—Juvenile literature.
Classification: LCC DK266 (ebook) | LCC DK266 .A58 2019 (print) | DDC
   947.085/4—dc23
LC record available at https://lccn.loc.gov/2017054542

Contents

Is slavery immoral?

No thinking person today would argue that slavery is moral. Yet in the United States in the early and mid-1800s, slavery was an accepted institution in the southern states. While many southerners never owned slaves, the institution of slavery had widespread support from plantation owners, elected officials, and even the general populace. Its defenders were often respected members of their communities. For instance, John C. Calhoun—a US senator from South Carolina—was a staunch defender of slavery. He believed that enslaved Africans benefited from their status as slaves—and said as much during an 1837 Senate speech. "Never before," he stated, "has the black race of Central Africa, from the dawn of history to the present day, attained a condition so civilized and so improved, not only physically, but morally and intellectually."

Statements like this might be confounding and hurtful today. But a true understanding of history—especially of those events that have altered daily life and human communities—requires students to become familiar with the thoughts, attitudes, and beliefs of the people who lived these events. Only by examining various perspectives will students truly understand the past and be able to make sound judgments about the future.

This is the goal of the *Debating History* series. Through a narrative-driven, pro/con format, the series introduces students to some of the complex issues that have dominated public discourse over the decades—topics such as the slave trade, twentieth-century immigration, the Soviet Union's collapse, and the rise of Islamist extremism. All chapters revolve around a single, pointed question, such as the following:

- Is slavery immoral?
- Do immigrants threaten American culture and values?
- Did the arms race cause the Soviet Union's collapse?
- Does poverty cause Islamist extremism?

This inquiry-based approach to history introduces student researchers to core issues and concerns on a given topic. Each chapter includes one part that argues the affirmative and one part that argues the negative—all written by a single author. With the single-author format, the predominant arguments for and against an issue can be synthesized into clear, accessible discussions supported by details and evidence, including relevant facts, quotes, and examples. All volumes include focus questions to guide students as they read each pro/con discussion, a visual chronology, and a list of sources for conducting further research.

This approach reflects the guiding principles set out in the College, Career, and Civic Life (C3) Framework for Social Studies State Standards developed by the National Council for the Social Studies. "History is interpretive," the framework's authors write. "Even if they are eyewitnesses, people construct different accounts of the same event, which are shaped by their perspectives—their ideas, attitudes, and beliefs. Historical understanding requires recognizing this multiplicity of points of view in the past. . . . It also requires recognizing that perspectives change over time, so that historical understanding requires developing a sense of empathy with people in the past whose perspectives might be very different from those of today." The *Debating History* series supports these goals by providing a solid introduction to the study of pro/con issues in history.

Important Events in the Collapse of the Soviet Union

1980
The United States initiates a grain embargo against the Soviet Union and boycotts the Moscow Olympic Games.

1983
Andropov, recognizing the weakness of the Soviet economy, undertakes limited economic reforms.

1984
Andropov dies and is replaced by Konstantin Chernenko, a hard-line politician who is in poor health.

| 1980 | 1981 | 1982 | 1983 | 1984 | 1985 |

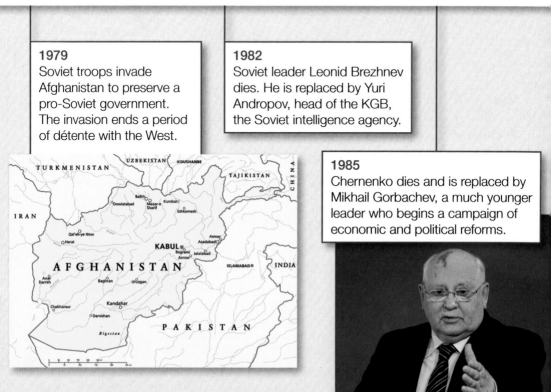

1979
Soviet troops invade Afghanistan to preserve a pro-Soviet government. The invasion ends a period of détente with the West.

1982
Soviet leader Leonid Brezhnev dies. He is replaced by Yuri Andropov, head of the KGB, the Soviet intelligence agency.

1985
Chernenko dies and is replaced by Mikhail Gorbachev, a much younger leader who begins a campaign of economic and political reforms.

1986
The nuclear power plant at Chernobyl explodes. Under Gorbachev's policy of glasnost, the Soviet Union releases information about the accident.

1999
With the nation gripped by high unemployment and rampant corruption, Yeltsin resigns as Russian president and names Vladimir Putin as his successor.

1991
The Congress of People's Deputies votes to dissolve the Soviet Union. Russia, Ukraine, and Belarus set up the Commonwealth of Independent States. Gorbachev resigns as president; Yeltsin is elected new leader of the Russian Federation.

1988
At a special meeting of the Communist Party, Soviet officials agree to allow a private sector in the economy.

1986   **1988**   **1990**   **1992**   **1994**   **1996**   **1998**

1987
The Soviet Union and the United States agree to eliminate intermediate-range nuclear missiles; Gorbachev's political rival Boris Yeltsin is removed as Moscow party boss for his criticisms about the slow pace of reform.

1992
Yeltsin embarks on a program of free-market economic reforms. Russian oligarchs begin to gain control of the nation's industries.

1990
The Soviet Union allows its republics to become independent with a two-thirds majority referendum vote. Yeltsin helps foil a coup attempt by military and intelligence hard-liners.

1989
The Berlin Wall falls and Communist regimes topple in Eastern and central Europe. Soviet troops exit Afghanistan.

Chapter One

A Brief History of the Soviet Union's Collapse

In August 1991 almost 1 million pro-democracy Russians flooded the Moscow streets to prevent a military coup against Soviet leader Mikhail Gorbachev. Hard-line elements of the KGB, the Soviet intelligence service, sought to end Gorbachev's program of widespread reforms. The hard-liners were holding Gorbachev prisoner inside his Crimean vacation home while they sent tanks and troops to take over the Soviet parliament in Moscow. A huge mass of street protesters managed to thwart the chaotic takeover attempt. Three young protesters lost their lives in the fighting.

Twenty-five years later a much smaller crowd gathered in central Moscow on the anniversary of the foiled coup. They met to pay tribute to those who fought against the last-ditch effort to preserve Communist tyranny. Meanwhile, a number of riot police stood nearby. Moscow City Hall had originally denied all permits for this annual tribute, having relented only at the last minute. Soviet president Vladimir Putin was determined to prevent the outbreak of any large-scale pro-democracy protests. Putin himself is a former KGB agent who deplores what he considers the tragedy of the Soviet Union's collapse. "Putin is the heir of those KGB-linked officials that planned the coup," says Mikhail Schneider, a member of an opposition group. "The anniversary of the defeat of the coup is not a holiday for him."[1] In fact, the collapse of the Soviet Union remains one of the most controversial episodes of the late twentieth century.

A Fateful Invasion

Many historians mark the beginnings of the collapse as December 1979, when thousands of Soviet troops invaded neighboring Afghanistan. It was the first time the Soviets had intervened in a country outside its eastern bloc of subject nations. Soviet leaders sought to stem a dangerous civil war threatening to overthrow the Afghan government, which was Communist and already existed under Soviet influence. Many Muslims in Afghanistan were rebelling against the government's policies, such as collectivization of land use and agriculture, which they saw as contrary to the tenets of Islam. The Soviets intervened because of their long-standing aim to preserve Communist regimes anywhere in the world. This policy, known as the Brezhnev Doctrine, for Soviet leader Leonid Brezhnev, had guided Cold War strategy in the Kremlin (the Russian version of the White House) for years. The Cold War was a global struggle for influence between the United States and the Soviet Union, a contest that avoided all-out warfare between the two nuclear powers.

The Soviet invasion brought worldwide condemnation. A decade of détente, or easing of tensions, with the United States and the West quickly fell to a new era of Cold War confrontation. President Jimmy Carter imposed a series of sanctions in response. He withdrew from Senate consideration the SALT II nuclear arms agreement he had made with Brezhnev. Carter also stopped American grain sales to the Soviet Union, threatened to end other trade pacts, and announced a US boycott of the 1980 Olympic Games in Moscow. Ronald Reagan defeated Carter in the 1980 presidential election with promises to build up US forces, both conventional and nuclear, and oppose Soviet expansion. Thus, the invasion of Afghanistan led to the worst period of US-Soviet relations since the 1960s.

The Soviet Union was confident that the United States would not interfere with its military action against the Afghan rebels. Yet although the United States did not employ its own forces, it did help arm the rebel guerrilla fighters—known as the mujahideen, or soldiers of God—with a variety of weapons. Among these were shoulder-mounted Stinger surface-to-air missiles, which targeted Soviet helicopters with deadly accuracy. Soviet forces soon became mired in a conflict many observers compared to America's involvement in Vietnam.

As the war dragged on, it became a perilous drain on Soviet resources in money and personnel. The increasing numbers of dead and wounded soldiers returning to the various republics of the Union of Soviet Socialist Republics (USSR) could not be hidden from the people. By the mid-1980s, anger at the Soviet government's war policy, along with protests related to human rights, led some dissidents to air their grievances against Communist rule. Although the Soviets jailed many of these critics or sentenced them to internal exile far from their homes, the protests continued to grow. According to Robert F. Baumann, former director at the US Army Command and General Staff College at Fort Leavenworth in Kansas, "The anguish of the war in Afghanistan deepened emerging fissures in Soviet society and contributed to its eventual disintegration."[2]

> "The anguish of the war in Afghanistan deepened emerging fissures in Soviet society and contributed to its eventual disintegration."[2]
>
> —Robert F. Baumann, former director at the US Army Command and General Staff College at Fort Leavenworth in Kansas

The Rise of Gorbachev

The Reagan administration's aggressive arms buildup left little doubt that the Cold War was heating up once more. Soviet leaders responded by shoring up their nuclear forces, but spending on

The Soviet Sphere of Influence Expands in Eastern Europe

1945: After World War II, Russia/Soviet Union extends its influence
1949–1989: Russia/Soviet Union sphere of influence expands even farther
European countries that do not fall under Russian/Soviet influence

*Until 1968
Note: Map uses modern European borders.

Afghanistan ruled out large increases in other military programs. Overall, the Soviet economy was ailing. Oil, one of the main Soviet exports, was falling in price and value. The faulty system of central planning—in which the Politburo (the Soviet ruling committee) made all key economic decisions for the nation, including manufacturing quotas and distribution of resources—could not meet the people's demands for everyday consumer goods. Soviet leaders from Brezhnev, who died in 1982, to Yuri Andropov and Konstantin Chernenko were aging men who seemed lacking in energy and new ideas. Following Chernenko's death in 1985, the

Politburo chose fifty-four-year-old Mikhail Gorbachev as general secretary. Known as a rising star in the Communist Party, Gorbachev immediately introduced sweeping reforms aimed at reviving the economy and gaining the people's support.

Gorbachev believed that fixing the Soviet economy required major changes in the nation's political and social structure. To achieve these changes, he embarked on two main reform efforts. Perestroika, which means "restructuring," sought to reorganize the economy and make it run more efficiently by adding free-market ideas to the system of central planning. It also urged a new focus on order and discipline among workers. Campaigns against drunkenness, idleness, and shoddy work habits filled newspapers and airwaves. Glasnost, or openness, eased restrictions on certain publications and broadcasts and allowed open debates about Soviet history and current affairs. Reports of Joseph Stalin's forced famines and bloody purges of the 1930s were aired in public for the first time. Gorbachev himself referred to government crimes in speeches to the nation. Conventional wisdom was upended so rapidly that one year (1988) school history exams were canceled because the textbooks, as school officials finally acknowledged, were riddled with lies. Gorbachev also released political prisoners, such as the dissident nuclear physicist Andrei Sakharov. Observers in the West, amazed at the pace of change, hailed Gorbachev as a new kind of Soviet ruler.

Gorbachev's reforms at home led to hopes for a breakthrough in arms control talks. Reagan, an outspoken opponent of communism, had labeled the Soviet Union "an evil empire"[3] and predicted that Communist regimes would end up "on the ash-heap of history."[4] Yet despite this rhetoric, summit meetings between Gorbachev and Reagan were actually productive. The two leaders charmed each other and found many areas of agreement. In 1986, at their second meeting in Reykjavik, Iceland, they discussed eliminating nuclear weapons altogether. The talks broke down, however, on Reagan's refusal to abandon the Strategic Defense Initiative (SDI), a proposed space-based missile defense system. Mocked by the world press as "Star Wars," the system nonetheless alarmed Gorbachev as a potential end to the balance of power. Although SDI never went beyond the drawing board, the Soviets considered it proof that the United States was outdistancing them in military technology. Even before the Reykjavik summit, Gorbachev had told his advisers, "If they impose a second round of arms race upon us, we will lose."[5]

Collapse of an Empire

In the next few years, the Soviet Union fell apart—gradually at first and then suddenly. Perestroika and its attempts to make the economy work more efficiently could not solve the core problems with centralized control. While many Western analysts lauded Soviet successes in expanding productivity, the truth was that the Soviet economy was only one-third as large as that of its American rival. Spending on the Soviet military was unsustainable, at 30 percent to 40 percent of GDP—or gross domestic product—the total money value of all goods and services produced by a nation in a certain period, usually one year. Gorbachev's policy of openness began to shake the foundations of the authoritarian Soviet state. Glasnost revelations of Soviet misdeeds led citizens in the satellite nations of the Warsaw Pact to mount more vigorous antigovernment protests. (The Warsaw Pact was a Soviet-led military alliance of communist nations in Eastern Europe. The North Atlantic Treaty Organization, or NATO, is a similar alliance of western democracies led by the United States.) In Poland the Solidarity labor union movement and its allies swept elections over the Communists. Polish opposition leader Adam Michnik said, "Were it not for the 'perestroika virus,' our [democratic movement] could not have got where it is today."[6] Events began to spin out of Gorbachev's control.

> "Were it not for the 'perestroika virus,' our [democratic movement] could not have got where it is today."[6]
>
> —Polish opposition leader Adam Michnik

On the night of November 9, 1989, crowds of Germans wielding hammers and pickaxes began to tear down the Berlin Wall, the barrier that had separated East and West Berlin since 1961. By choosing not to intervene, Gorbachev essentially admitted that the Cold War was over. Germany, divided into Communist East Germany and democratic West Germany after World War II, set about to reunite, and other nations of Eastern Europe made plans for independence.

Momentum for democracy led Gorbachev to allow multiparty elections and establish a presidency for the Soviet Union, an office he assumed in 1990. But his support among the people faltered as the economy failed to improve. Hard-line Communists in the Politburo blamed Gorbachev for the dissolution of the Soviet empire and the general sense of chaos. In December 1991, a few months after the hard-liners' coup attempt, Gorbachev resigned as president, and the Soviet Union collapsed for good. Boris Yeltsin, a regional party boss who had become a political rival to Gorbachev, assumed leadership of Russia and promptly dismantled the Communist Party apparatus. Russian historian Valery Solovei gives Gorbachev credit for the Soviet Union breaking apart with relatively little bloodshed. "He wanted better," says Solovei. "Now people in Russia hate him. Very often I think he looks like King Lear from Shakespeare, who lost his kingdom. And Gorbachev lost his kingdom, too."[7]

Chapter Two

Was the Soviet Invasion of Afghanistan a Key Factor in the Soviet Union's Collapse?

The Soviet Invasion of Afghanistan Was Not a Key Factor in the Soviet Union's Collapse

- The Afghanistan war was a minor conflict that had limited impact on the Soviet economy.
- Despite its enemy's claims, the Soviets did not lose the war but decided to withdraw when it ground down to a stalemate.
- For most of the war, Soviet leadership was able to conceal from its citizens the problems its military was facing in Afghanistan.
- The number of Soviet soldiers killed or wounded in the conflict, while significant, was not disastrous.

The Debate at a Glance

The Soviet Invasion of Afghanistan Was a Key Factor in the Soviet Union's Collapse

- The costly, drawn-out invasion put a great strain on the already weak Soviet economy.
- The war in Afghanistan drew increasing criticism from Soviet citizens under the new policies of glasnost and open dissent.
- Failure in Afghanistan showed that the Soviet Union could no longer put down uprisings in its neighboring states, undermining the Stalin-era myth of invincibility.

The Soviet Invasion of Afghanistan Was Not a Key Factor in the Soviet Union's Collapse

"Afghanistan increasingly looked like a long war, but for a 5-million strong Soviet military force the losses there were negligible. . . . The cost of the Afghan war itself was hardly crushing: Estimated at $4 billion to $5 billion in 1985, it was an insignificant portion of the Soviet GDP."

—Leon Aron, director of Russian studies at the American Enterprise Institute

Leon Aron, "Everything You Think You Know About the Collapse of the Soviet Union Is Wrong," *Foreign Policy*, June 20, 2011. http://foreignpolicy.com.

Consider these questions as you read:

1. Do you agree that comparisons between the Soviet war in Afghanistan and the US war in Vietnam are greatly overstated? Explain.
2. Was the Brezhnev Doctrine a realistic policy in the modern world? Why or why not?
3. When you consider how important it was for the Soviets to control information about the war, do you think they succeeded in this objective? Explain.

Editor's note: The discussion that follows presents common arguments made in support of this perspective. All arguments are supported by facts, quotes, and examples taken from various sources of the period or present day.

The Soviet invasion of neighboring Afghanistan began as a minor intervention aimed at propping up a Communist regime under attack from rebel forces. Although the conflict dragged on for a decade—much longer than Soviet officials anticipated at first—it never threatened the overall stability of the Soviet government. Many historians compare the Soviet war in Afghanistan to America's disastrous involvement in Vietnam. They blame the Afghan war for placing too heavy a burden on the Soviet economy. They argue that the conflict revealed the weakness of the Soviet military. They suggest the war created an angry opposition movement and ultimately destabilized the whole Soviet system of government. However, these claims are wildly overstated.

From the Soviet point of view, the invasion was necessary. The new regime based in Kabul, Afghanistan's capital, had arisen in spring of 1978 via a coup by the Communist People's Democratic Party of Afghanistan. The coup, while not Moscow's work, put in place a pro-Soviet government much to the Kremlin's liking. However, in September 1979 Nur Mohammed Taraki, who the coup leaders had installed as president, was murdered by his bodyguards and replaced by Hafizullah Amin. A violent leader, Amin faced opposition from two-thirds of the country, including rural peasants and urban intellectuals. His bloody reprisals and mass executions threw Afghanistan into a violent revolt. According to author and historian Rupert Colley, "the new situation in Afghanistan demanded a rethink within the Kremlin, which concluded that the toppling of Taraki's pro-Soviet regime set a bad example which could be repeated elsewhere in the communist world and that a show of force was needed."[8] On December 27, with Amin's rule hanging by a thread, Soviet leaders decided to act. They sent in a force of about forty thousand to seize control of cities and highways. Soviet troops stormed the palace in Kabul, shot Amin (found cowering behind a bar), and replaced him with Babrak Karmal, formerly an Afghan diplomat.

Like the Soviet interventions in Hungary in 1956 and Czechoslovakia in 1968, the Afghan invasion followed the logic of the Brezhnev Doctrine: No regime in the Soviet sphere would be allowed to break free from the Communist yoke. "The Brezhnev Doctrine is the moment Soviet policy went from verbal to outright physical threats," notes British historian Robert Wilde, "the moment the USSR said it would invade anyone who stepped out of its line."[9] Thus, the Soviets viewed the Afghan invasion as a short-term task to be handled with ruthless efficiency. Outraged protests from world leaders were irksome but to be expected.

Moscow considered the operation a strong message to Communist states that straying from Soviet influence would have swift consequences. Soviet planners also hoped to gain a foothold in southwestern Asia and stem the tide of radical Islam from Iran and other Middle Eastern states. Confident in the strength of their own nation, the Soviets saw few downsides in shoring up the Afghan government until its armed forces could take over the fight against the rebels.

Not an Economic Disaster

Certainly the mujahideen surprised Soviet commanders with their abilities as guerrilla fighters in villages and the countryside. As the conflict dragged on, their fierce resistance—and the failings of the Afghan military—led the Soviets to raise troop numbers to nearly 120,000 and increase spending on bombing raids, tanks, helicopters, and troop support. Yet total Soviet spending on the war, while considerable, was far from being a disaster economically. In 1987 the CIA reported:

> The war has not been a substantial drain on the Soviet economy so far, although the costs of the war have been rising faster than total defense spending. We estimate that from their initial invasion in December 1979 through 1986 the Soviets have spent about 15 billion rubles on the conduct of the war. . . . Measured in dollars—what it would have cost the United States to procure, operate, and maintain the same force in Afghanistan—we estimate that the total cost through the seven years of the war has

been less than $50 billion. This is only 75 percent of what the war in Vietnam cost the United States in the peak year of 1968.[10]

By 1985 the Soviet army and its Afghan guerrilla adversaries had reached a standoff. As the Soviets increasingly transferred battlefield responsibilities to the Afghan army, they continued to pour billions into the war effort. This placed some strain on the Soviet economy but did not create a downturn overall. In fact,

Afghan mujahideen fighters rest during operations against Soviet invaders in 1980. The Afghans' guerrilla tactics mired the enemy in a long, costly war. In 1988, after more than eight years of conflict, the toll in men, money, and reputation convinced the Kremlin to withdraw.

in the early years of the war, the Soviet economy actually grew slightly. By 1989, with Gorbachev's economic reforms in full swing, spending on the war remained at a level most economists still considered manageable. According to Leon Aron, director of Russian studies at the American Enterprise Institute, the war certainly did not wreck the Soviet economy. "The Soviet Union had known far greater calamities and coped without sacrificing an iota of the state's grip on society and economy, much less surrendering it,"[11] says Aron. Those who claim the war was the main cause of the sagging Soviet economy are mistaken.

Stalemate, Not Defeat

The notion that the Soviet army suffered a humiliating defeat at the hands of the mujahideen is another misconception about the war. Like American forces in Vietnam, the Soviets fought an enemy well versed in guerrilla tactics to a bitter stalemate. Thus, conclusions about how Afghanistan exposed the weakness of the Soviet military—and by extension the whole Soviet system—are mistaken. Jonathan Steele, author of *Ghosts of Afghanistan: Hard Truths and Foreign Myths*, explains:

> The reality is the Afghan mujahideen did not defeat the Soviets on the battlefield. They won some important encounters, notably in the Panjshir valley, but lost others. In sum, neither side defeated the other. The Soviets could have remained in Afghanistan for several more years but they decided to leave when Gorbachev calculated that the war had become a stalemate and was no longer worth the high price in men, money and international prestige.[12]

Another myth, says Steele, is that the shoulder-fired Stinger missiles provided by the CIA for attacks on Soviet helicopters actually turned the war in favor of the rebels. The Soviet decision to leave Afghanistan was made in October 1985, months before the Stinger missiles arrived in bulk. Once the rebels did employ them, Soviet helicopter pilots responded by flying more often at night and at higher altitudes. Notes from meetings of the Politburo (the Soviet ruling body) show no particular concern about use of Stinger missiles or any other mujahideen tactic. The Soviet military remained a formidable force throughout the 1980s and did not flee Afghanistan in a state of disarray.

Control of Information

Many analysts suggest that reports about the Soviet Union's military problems in Afghanistan led to mounting protests and helped undermine the Soviet state. But this view underestimates the Communist government's ability to withhold information and manipulate public opinion about ongoing events.

After all, this was a society that still had not learned the truth about Stalin's crimes, which had been perpetrated decades ago. It was three days after the invasion of Afghanistan before the Soviet public got the news. They were assured, falsely, that the Afghan government had requested Soviet assistance. For the entire first year of the occupation, Soviet officials denied their forces had suffered any casualties. The first Soviet death in Afghanistan was announced only in 1981. As the war progressed, no casualty lists were published, and few names of dead soldiers were released to the public. "To hide the existence of casualties, the Soviets initially evacuated most of their wounded to Eastern Europe," says historian J. Bruce Amstutz. "To hide casualties further, the Soviets stopped shipping bodies back to the Soviet Union, supposedly burying

> "The reality is the Afghan mujahideen did not defeat the Soviets on the battlefield."[12]
>
> —Jonathan Steele, author of *Ghosts of Afghanistan: Hard Truths and Foreign Myths*

them in Afghanistan."[13] Soviet officials claimed less than fourteen thousand dead by the time their troops pulled out, a number that was significant but low compared to every other war the Red Army had fought going back to the 1920s.

In pursuit of secrecy, the Soviets used recruits mainly from the Baltic Sea area and from small villages in non-Russian republics. News about military setbacks was slow to seep out to the wider populace. There were some small protests in Soviet cities, but nothing remotely like the massive antiwar demonstrations in Vietnam-era America. By the mid-1980s dissatisfaction among Soviet citizens was real and growing. However, the war in Afghanistan contributed little fuel to this unrest and played only a marginal role in the Soviet Union's eventual collapse.

The Soviet Invasion of Afghanistan Was a Key Factor in the Soviet Union's Collapse

"For almost 10 years, Moscow had to carry on a war unsupportable by the government, a conflict that brought about the demoralization and finally the breakup of the Soviet empire."

—Zbigniew Brzezinski, national security adviser to Jimmy Carter, in a 1998 interview with *Le Nouvel Observateur*

Quoted in Centre for Research on Globalization, "The CIA's Intervention in Afghanistan: Interview with Zbigniew Brzezinski," October 15, 2001. www.globalresearch.ca.

Consider these questions as you read:

1. Do you think Soviet leaders were surprised by the global reaction to the invasion of Afghanistan? Explain.
2. Could ethnic tensions among Soviet troops have been avoided? What do they indicate about the state of the Soviet Union?
3. Do you agree that the Soviet invasion of Afghanistan played a major role in the Soviet Union's collapse? Why or why not?

Editor's note: The discussion that follows presents common arguments made in support of this perspective. All arguments are supported by facts, quotes, and examples taken from various sources of the period or present day.

The collapse of the Soviet Union is often attributed to failures of leadership and weaknesses in a central planning system that was equal parts inept and corrupt. Yet the Soviet war in Afghanistan was certainly another crucial factor in the breakdown. In 1979, when the invasion began, the Soviet Union was regarded as a legitimate superpower. It was considered roughly equal in military might and global influence to its Cold War foe, the United States. The Soviet economy, while smaller than that of the United States, was thought to be fairly strong and stable, offering proof that socialist central planning could produce steady growth. The Soviet political system, with its emphasis on collective solutions, was touted by sympathetic observers in the West as a valid alternative to capitalist democracy. However, the war in Afghanistan helped shatter all these assumptions. Perception was overturned by a new reality. By the time the Soviet Union withdrew all troops in 1989, its military prowess, economic strength, and even status as a superpower were being called into question. Unforeseen cracks began to emerge in the Soviet system.

The invasion proved disastrous in several ways, with the political fallout affecting the Soviet economy. In the attempt to prop up an unpopular government in Kabul, the Soviets lost support worldwide among those opposed to imperialism. "By sending in its army to fight a popular revolt [the Soviet Union] isolated itself internationally and was portrayed as a predatory imperial power," says Patrick Cockburn, a journalist who covered the Soviet war in Afghanistan. "All the obloquy [scorn] which had been loaded on the US over the Vietnam War in the 1960s and 1970s was now directed at the Soviet Union in the 1980s."[14] At the time, the Soviets needed détente with the United States and Western Europe for its economic advantages. Reduced tensions had allowed for less military spending and the lure of trade deals with the West. After the Afghanistan invasion, the Soviet Union instead faced American embargoes on grain and fertilizer and stiff sanctions on trade and technology. These helped weaken its economy and sowed discord among its people. The Afghanistan war set in motion a downward spiral that the Kremlin ultimately could not control.

A Long and Expensive War

The Soviet war in Afghanistan became a strategic quagmire putting tremendous strain on the already weak Soviet economy. Spending for the war consumed billions of dollars each year, as Kremlin planners poured men and equipment into the country to defeat the mujahideen. As a result, Soviet military spending rose from 33 percent of GDP in 1980 to 39 percent in 1985, when Mikhail Gorbachev assumed leadership. By the end of the decade, that percentage would rise to an unsustainable 47 percent.

The war's ruinous cost forced Gorbachev's hand. Referring to the war as "the bleeding wound,"[15] he made ending the conflict a top priority. By the mid-1980s the Soviet economy had almost completely stopped growing. Production in previously strong industries like coal and steel continued to decline. Diverting funds to the war effort left even less available for producing the consumer goods demanded by a growing urban middle class. The costly war also made it much more difficult for the Soviet Union to maintain its large armies elsewhere in the republics. The mounting arms race with the United States created a further strain on the budget. Gorbachev's perestroika reforms—desperate measures amounting almost to shock therapy—were designed to improve efficiency and give the economy an immediate boost. Instead, they proved much less effective than hoped. Urban Russians and the non-Russian populations in the various republics had at first supported Gorbachev's reform program. But by 1988 they began to lose faith that real change was at hand. Many blamed what they saw as a needless war in Afghanistan. As the Turkish historian Anil Cicek notes:

> "The economic resources that were spent for the continuation of the war were so great that this sum could have created a boosting effect had it rather been spent for the structural reforms needed in the Soviet economy."[16]
>
> —Turkish historian Anil Cicek

The economic resources that were spent for the continuation of the war were so great that this sum could have created a boosting effect had it rather been spent for the structural reforms needed in the Soviet economy.

An effective transformation in the economy could also have increased productivity and thus could have helped the Soviet leadership meet the increasing material needs of the non-Russian minorities.[16]

Thus, the Afghanistan war blunted the effectiveness of Gorbachev's reforms. What started as a limited invasion to support a puppet Communist regime mushroomed into an economic disaster.

Criticism of the War and Glasnost

As the Afghan occupation dragged on, it also brought open dissent all across the Soviet Union. Criticism began in the early 1980s. Soviet attempts to censor the news regarding casualty numbers and battlefield results could not block out the reality of the war. With the conflict escalating, Soviet casualties increased.

Soviet armored personnel carriers begin the slow retreat from Afghanistan in 1988. The strong, well-equipped Soviet army had been fought to a stalemate by guerrilla forces. The decision to withdraw reflected poorly on the Soviet military and Moscow's international standing.

Disabled and mutilated soldiers began returning to their home-towns in numbers impossible to ignore. Despite official censor-ship, stories about these soldiers appeared on television and in newspapers. Soviet officials dismissed claims that Afghanistan veterans—known as *Afgantsy*—were receiving little government help in obtaining housing and health care. The Afgantsy them-selves started to speak out about their neglect.

Dissent over the war had a strong ethnic basis. Most of the Afgantsy came from non-Russian Soviet republics. They resent-ed bearing the brunt of the fighting while Russian soldiers mainly served in leadership roles. Troops from Asian regions of the Soviet Union were sometimes reluctant to fire on the Afghans, whom they viewed as virtual kinsmen, and some of these Asians chose to desert. A few captured soldiers even changed sides. As Soviet losses grew, commanders questioned the resolve of their central Asian troops. Mixed Soviet units made up of various nationalities began to fight among themselves. There were also stories of drug abuse, looting, and smuggling in the ranks, along with accounts of atrocities committed in the field. Reports of trouble subduing the mujahideen raised alarms throughout the Soviet Union, where the populace had come to regard the Red Army as invincible. The Afgantsy and their ethnic neighbors who once would have held their tongues in fear began to engage in open criticism of Mos-cow and the war. In this way the Afghanistan war was a divisive event that weakened Moscow's central authority.

Gorbachev's glasnost policy of freer information and more open debate only served to increase the protests. Throughout the Soviet Union, antimilitary feelings grew stronger. Leaked reports about corruption and war crimes among Soviet troops filled the Soviet media. The government's official version of events lost cred-ibility. Moscow's decision to abandon the war effort was perceived as an embarrassing defeat. The Red Army, an object of national pride since World War II, lost face at home and in the eyes of the world. According to political scientists Rafael Reuveny and Aseem Prakash, "Since the Soviet army was the glue that held the diverse

Soviet Republics together, its defeat in Afghanistan had profound implications for the survivability of the Soviet Union."[17]

Military Failure and Disintegration

The Soviet military's failure in Afghanistan led to separatist movements in the non-Russian republics. Locals understood that the Soviet army lacked discipline and unity. Resistance to Moscow and Communist Party rule no longer seemed impossible. By 1989 there were antimilitary protests outside army bases in Lithuania, Latvia, and Georgia. Resistance to the draft was widespread. Protesters carried signs that accused the Red Army of being an occupation force and perpetrating war crimes. The army no longer held legitimacy as the glue of the Communist Party and the champion of the oppressed. As a result, the Afgantsy and others organized into political groups separate from the ruling Communists. Films and popular songs portrayed the plight of the Afgantsy, who were widely seen as victims of the government's incompetence and lack of sympathy.

> "Since the Soviet army was the glue that held the diverse Soviet Republics together, its defeat in Afghanistan had profound implications for the survivability of the Soviet Union."[17]
>
> —Political scientists Rafael Reuveny and Aseem Prakash

From the start, the Soviet Union consisted of many different ethnic and national groups held together by respect for (or fear of) the military and the Communist Party. When the Afghanistan war wrecked the army's reputation, the center could not hold. Fissures opened between the military and civilians, Russians and non-Russians, Communist true believers and weary realists. Gorbachev's decision not to send the Red Army to defend the Berlin Wall convinced the outlying republics to pursue their own freedom. Sergei Lukyanchikov, director of *Pain*, a documentary about Afghanistan, said, "The War changed our psychology. It helped *perestroika*."[18] It also helped bring down the Soviet Union.

Chapter Three

Did the Arms Race Cause the Soviet Union's Collapse?

The Arms Race Led Directly to the Soviet Union's Collapse

- The Reagan administration's rejection of détente and use of labels to demonize the Soviet Union made a new arms race inevitable.
- The economic superiority of the United States enabled it to pursue an arms race that the Soviet Union could not hope to win.
- The arms race revealed the underlying weakness of the Soviet economy and made social tensions worse.

The Debate at a Glance

The Arms Race Did Not Cause the Soviet Union's Collapse

- Gorbachev was more interested in reforming the Soviet political system and economy than in expanding its military.
- In pursuing his reforms, Gorbachev had to deal with hard-line elements among the Soviet leadership that were dedicated to the arms race and preserving the empire.
- Later cuts in Soviet defense spending did not indicate a surrender in the arms race but rather a new emphasis on the Soviet economy.

The Arms Race Led Directly to the Soviet Union's Collapse

"Behind all this [talk about the Strategic Defense Initiative] lies the clear calculation that the USSR will exhaust its material resources before the U.S.A. and therefore be forced to surrender."

—Soviet foreign minister Andrei Gromyko in his first meeting with US president Ronald Reagan in 1984

Kim R. Holmes, *Rebound: Getting America Back to Great.* Lanham, MD: Rowman & Littlefield, 2013, p. 71.

Consider these questions as you read:

1. Do you believe that Reagan's arms buildup was the main cause of the Soviet Union's collapse? Why or why not?
2. Do you agree that the Soviet Union presented a deadly military threat to the West? Why or why not?
3. Were the Soviets foolish to take the threat from the Strategic Defense Initiative so seriously? Explain.

Editor's note: The discussion that follows presents common arguments made in support of this perspective. All arguments are supported by facts, quotes, and examples taken from various sources of the period or present day.

It was the Soviet Union's misfortune that Ronald Reagan entered the White House in January 1981 with a new plan to win the Cold War. Reagan was determined to remedy America's loss of confidence after the catastrophe of the Vietnam War. He aimed to strengthen America's military, including its strategic nuclear forces. The military buildup would enable the United States to challenge Soviet expansion anywhere in the world. It would also ensure that any arms talks would always be conducted from a position of strength. With its renewed military might, the United States would once again be able to exert moral leadership in the world. It could promote freedom and democracy for nations that might be wavering under the lure of communism. Reagan, whom his critics at home and abroad considered a naive and rather simpleminded idealist, had a knack for expressing his goals in blunt terms. "Here's my strategy on the Cold War," he once explained, "we win, they lose."[19]

Such pronouncements made Reagan's political opponents furious. As for Soviet officials, they publicly dismissed his words as empty bluster, but in private they paid heed. The Soviet Union had undertaken its own huge military buildup in the 1970s—diverting one-fourth of the nation's GDP to its forces. In the Soviets' own estimation, this left the balance of power in the Cold War tipped in their favor. By 1979, while the United States was suffering the humiliation of its embassy takeover in Iran, Soviet influence was spreading rapidly. Developing countries at the United Nations voted as an anti-American, pro-Soviet bloc that supported the aims of socialism, anti-imperialism, and revolution. Soviet-style communism, with its reliance on authoritarian government seizing control of the economy and culture in the name of the people, was embraced by certain Latin American countries, while the Red Army's invasion of Afghanistan promised a possible opening to the Middle East. Strategically, the Soviet Union seemed to be in a dominant position. But now this new American president with his longtime hatred of communism was openly threatening to oppose Soviet advances anywhere in the world.

The existential threat Reagan saw in the Soviets—a threat to the very existence of the West's democracies—was no mirage. The USSR commanded a potent military on land and in water. Its Red Army boasted vast numbers of troops, tanks, and artillery. Its submarine fleet was the largest in the world. Its surface ships were floating arsenals. It also maintained a first-strike nuclear force with more missiles than the United States. Documents released since the end of the Cold War show that the Kremlin was contemplating a massive invasion of Western Europe, in which Warsaw Pact tanks and troops would pour over the borders. The Soviets had made plans to use nuclear weapons against the United States

31

and certain European cities to prevent a counterattack. "These [war plans] were decidedly offensive [in] nature and envisioned a blitzkrieg-type assault that allowed the Warsaw Pact to conquer most of Western Europe in a matter of days," notes security expert Zachary Keck. "It amazingly sought to integrate the liberal use of nuclear weapons with the Warsaw Pact's formidable conventional military might."[20] The United States and its NATO allies had their own joint plans to drop nuclear bombs on the Soviet Union in the event of an attack. As crazy as these schemes sound today, they serve to emphasize what was at stake in the Cold War and why the arms race was a crucial component.

Aggressive New Policies

From his first days in office, Reagan shifted the strategy of the United States from coexisting with the Soviet Union to winning the Cold War outright. He rejected the policy of détente, much as his predecessor, Jimmy Carter, had after the Soviet invasion of Afghanistan. Unlike Carter, however, Reagan pulled no punches in his anti-Soviet rhetoric. In his very first press conference, he condemned Soviet leaders for having "openly and publicly declared that the only morality they recognize is what will further their cause, meaning they reserve unto themselves the right to commit any crime, to lie, to cheat, in order to attain that."[21] Later, he would call the Soviet Union an evil empire. Such statements were used to justify the massive arms buildup Reagan proceeded to push through Congress. Reagan also ordered his national security team to develop covert tactics to undermine Soviet control in Eastern and central Europe and disrupt the Soviet economy.

The bellicose language coming from the White House could not fail to draw a response from Moscow. Soviet generals and military strategists began calling for upgrades in missile technology and weapons systems. Despite increased spending on the war in Afghanistan, Soviet leaders from Leonid Brezhnev to Mikhail Gorbachev continued to funnel money into their defense industries. They recognized that it was essential to maintain the military's loyalty whatever the cost. "As early as the 1970s some officials warned Leonid Brezhnev that the economy would stagnate if the military continued to consume such a disproportionate share of resources," write foreign policy analysts Richard Ned Lebow and Janice Gross Stein. "The [Soviet] General Secretary ignored their warnings, in large part because his authority depended on the support of a coalition in which defense and heavy industry were well represented."[22] Soviet military planners demanded the resources to compete with Reagan's expansion, and Brezhnev, setting the pattern for those who came after him, was only too happy to oblige.

> "As early as the 1970s some officials warned Leonid Brezhnev that the economy would stagnate if the military continued to consume such a disproportionate share of resources."[22]
>
> —Foreign policy analysts Richard Ned Lebow and Janice Gross Stein

An Unwinnable Arms Race

The superiority of the US economy enabled Reagan to pursue an arms race that the Soviet Union could not possibly win. In fact, Reagan considered his plan to boost the economy by cutting taxes and reducing inflation an important part of his strategy to win the Cold War. Once the US economy was on a more solid footing, he could afford to rebuild the American military. Under Reagan, US military spending climbed to 27 percent of the federal budget (from about 23 percent under Carter). Just to keep pace, the Soviet Union would have to spend close to 60 percent of its budget on its military, and much of that money would have to be diverted from domestic programs. Ordinary people would suffer the most, and public discontent was likely to grow.

In addition, Reagan's military advisers focused not on traditional arms (although funds for them increased as well) but on new, technologically advanced weapons. The B-1 bomber, M-1 Abrams tank, and F-15 fighter bomber outstripped their Soviet counterparts. Reagan also ordered tight restrictions on transferring technology to other countries, making it difficult for the Soviets to re-create the new systems.

Reagan's strategy owed a great deal to what he perceived as the Soviet Union's main weakness: the waste and inefficiency of its planned economy. He believed the true state of the Soviet economy was much worse than its official figures suggested. This view was supported by analysts at the CIA. Taking into account factory shutdowns, food lines, and depleted resources, the CIA reported that the Soviet Union could barely feed and clothe its own people.

The Dispute over Star Wars

In 1983 Reagan revealed the centerpiece of his proposed cutting-edge military technology: the Strategic Defense Initiative (SDI)—soon to be dubbed "Star Wars" by its detractors. It was a ground- and space-based missile defense system designed to shoot down nuclear missiles in midflight. Jay Keyworth, Reagan's science adviser on SDI, emphasized the need for such a system. "We have got a second-class nation," he said, referring to the Soviet Union, "virtually a developing nation, threatening the existence of the United States, threatening the entire free world. . . . I think it is a pretty frightening set of circumstances."[23]

A few years later SDI became a sticking point in arms control talks between the Soviets and the United States. Gorbachev, taking a cue from his generals, regarded

> "We have got a second-class nation, virtually a developing nation, threatening the existence of the United States, threatening the entire free world. . . . I think it is a pretty frightening set of circumstances."[23]
>
> —Jay Keyworth, President Ronald Reagan's science adviser on SDI

To counter nuclear missile strikes, the SDI proposal initially included energy weapons fired from satellites (upper left), space-based platforms (right), and ground batteries (lower left). The Soviet Union's fragile economy could not compete with this projected escalation of the arms race.

SDI as a serious threat to the Cold War balance of power. He demanded that the United States abandon its SDI research, but Reagan refused. The dispute seemed to mark a turning point in Gorbachev's thinking. He doubted his nation's ability—both technological and economic—to develop its own missile defense system. He saw that a full-scale attempt to match the US arms buildup, especially its advanced new weaponry, quite likely would ravage the Soviet Union's fragile economy and destabilize its political system. Gorbachev realized the limits of Soviet military power and decided to focus on his reform program in order to stimulate the economy. In 1989, when East Germany and other East European satellite states declared their independence, he chose not to intervene. Two years later, the non-Russian republics also broke away, effectively dissolving the Soviet Union. Reagan's prediction that Soviet communism would be left "on the ash-heap of history"[24] had come true.

The Arms Race Did Not Cause the Soviet Union's Collapse

"The Carter-Reagan military buildup did not defeat the Soviet Union. . . . Gorbachev's determination to reform an economy crippled by defense spending . . . fueled his persistent search for an accommodation with the West."

—Richard Ned Lebow and Janice Gross Stein, foreign policy analysts

Richard Ned Lebow and Janice Gross Stein, "Reagan and the Russians," *Atlantic Monthly*, February 1994. www.theatlantic.com.

Consider these questions as you read:

1. Do you agree that Gorbachev's antimilitarism was a key factor in the Soviet Union's collapse? Explain.
2. In your opinion, would a leader with more hard-line views than Gorbachev have been able to preserve the Soviet Union? Why or why not?
3. Gorbachev is widely considered a hero in the West. Why do you think this is so?

Editor's note: The discussion that follows presents common arguments made in support of this perspective. All arguments are supported by facts, quotes, and examples taken from various sources of the period or present day.

One fantasy about the end of the Cold War refuses to die. That is the notion that the arms race with the United States caused the Soviet Union's collapse. In this version of events, President Ronald Reagan's massive military buildup forced the Soviet Union to realize it could not compete economically with the United States. Reagan is presented as the lone Cold Warrior who perceived the truth about the Soviet Union's weak economy and shaky hold over its ethnic republics and satellite states in Eastern Europe. People who prefer their history in black and white are drawn to this attractive piece of fiction. However, the truth is much more complicated. And it requires less focus on Reagan's role than on the more important contribution of Soviet leader Mikhail Gorbachev. For it was Gorbachev's clear-sighted view of the limits of militarism that ultimately led to the breakup of the Soviet Union. At a Moscow press conference in 1988, Reagan himself downplayed his own role in ending Cold War tensions. "Mr. Gorbachev deserves most of the credit," Reagan acknowledged, "as the leader of this country."[25]

One way Reagan did help bring about change was to influence the Politburo to seek a new kind of leader. Reagan's aggressive anti-Communist stance seemed to require a different approach in Moscow. The Politburo rejected the choice of another old man with outdated ideas in favor of a younger, more vibrant individual in Gorbachev. Instead of rigid Stalinist thinking, Gorbachev offered a more open mind and fresh ideas. In his public speeches, he was not afraid to address problems rarely mentioned by Soviet officials, such as alcoholism, lack of productivity, and corruption. This approach startled his listeners with its refreshing honesty and helped gain their trust. Having worked his way up the ranks of the Communist Party, Gorbachev knew firsthand how entrenched apparatchiks (upper-ranking party members) relied on bribery and favoritism to maintain their privileges. He recognized that Socialist central planning lacked the efficiency needed to provide consumer goods to the rising urban middle class. And improving the Soviet economy remained his key objective.

A Fresh Outlook

Gorbachev brought this fresh outlook to the question of Soviet armaments as well. He secretly hoped to deemphasize military threats in Soviet foreign policy so that resources could be channeled into fixing the economy. However, in agreeing to arms control talks with the United States, he did not expect to find a willing partner in Reagan. In fact, Gorbachev considered Reagan to be not only a conservative but a political dinosaur. Likewise, Reagan expected Gorbachev to be a typical Communist leader—devious and seeking any kind of advantage. Nonetheless, at their first summit, the pair developed a mutual trust. Reagan found that British prime minister Margaret Thatcher had been correct in describing Gorbachev as someone with whom he could do business. Gorbachev seemed more of a European-style social democrat—a believer in free elections as well as socialism—rather than a hard-line Communist. "Reagan came quickly to recognize that Gorbachev's goals, far from being traditional, were downright revolutionary," says Strobe Talbott, an American foreign policy analyst. "He also saw that the transformation Gorbachev had in mind for his country would, if it came about, serve American interests."[26]

> "Reagan came quickly to recognize that Gorbachev's goals, far from being traditional, were downright revolutionary."[26]
>
> —Strobe Talbott, American foreign policy analyst

Gorbachev was equally surprised at Reagan's agenda. Instead of an adversary bent on continuing the arms race, Gorbachev discovered a potential partner who openly shared his goal of disarmament and peace. In their 1986 summit at Reykjavik, Iceland, the two leaders actually discussed eliminating nuclear weapons altogether. Although the arms control talks finally broke down over Reagan's cherished SDI initiative, they established that Gorbachev, unlike his predecessors, was willing to step back from life-or-death competition with the West. This new approach would have major consequences for the Cold War and the survival of the Soviet regime.

Dealing with the Hard-Liners

In negotiating arms control pacts with the United States, Gorbachev constantly had to consider his hard-line opponents in the Kremlin. While Reagan's main political foes in Washington, DC,

At their 1986 meeting in Iceland, President Reagan and General Secretary Gorbachev discovered that they shared an interest in global peace and nuclear disarmament. However, the talks broke down when Reagan made it clear that he would not halt progress on the SDI program.

were liberals who fretted about him starting a nuclear war, Gorbachev's opponents were militarists who feared he was too soft for the job. According to Rozanne Ridgway, who served under Reagan as assistant secretary of European and Canadian affairs: "I think Gorbachev, at every step, had to hold off people who did not agree with where he was taking the Soviet Union. They predicted the destruction of the Soviet Union. In fact, they were right; that was all to the good as it was a ridiculous and tragic system. However, there were many who wanted to stick with it and fought Gorbachev every step of the way."[27]

Gorbachev was willing to compromise on arms control and possible disarmament because of his fundamental disagreement with past Soviet policies. He came to believe that the United States, and the West in general, was much less hostile to the USSR than the hard-liners would acknowledge. This led him to question the old Brezhnev policies that focused on military solutions and spending on arms instead of compromise and diplomatic flexibility. According to a 1988 analysis by Bruce Parrott of the Johns Hopkins School of Advanced International Studies, "Gorbachev has encouraged a strategic reassessment that minimizes the theme of inherent Western aggressiveness, highlights the possibilities of East-West cooperation, and identifies the main military threat to the USSR as accidental nuclear war rather than premeditated Western attack."[28]

Gorbachev also took a second look at the Soviet Union's commitments in developing nations. This led to the withdrawal of Soviet troops from Afghanistan and less emphasis on supporting Communist governments in Africa and Latin America. These moves further alarmed the old-guard militarists in the Kremlin. They could understand Gorbachev seeking temporary breathing room to focus on shoring up the economy. But they feared that these changes would become permanent and that the Soviet Union would essentially surrender to the West. As Parrott foresaw, "If Gorbachev pushes further along this road, as seems likely, he will need great political skill to prevent the emergence of a dangerous coalition uniting skeptical party leaders with conservative soldiers and policemen who believe his strategy threatens the interests of the Soviet state."[29]

In the end it was just such an angry coalition that would attempt a coup against Gorbachev and his fellow reformers. Gorbachev's willingness to oppose the hard-liners and seek avenues of compromise, far more than the burdens of the arms race, led to his own downfall and that of the Soviet Union. "A split in society

> "Gorbachev has encouraged a strategic reassessment that minimizes the theme of inherent Western aggressiveness, highlights the possibilities of East-West cooperation, and identifies the main military threat to the USSR as accidental nuclear war rather than premeditated Western attack."[28]
>
> —Bruce Parrott, Johns Hopkins School of Advanced International Studies

and a struggle in a country like ours, overflowing with weapons, including nuclear ones, could have left so many people dead and caused such destruction," says Gorbachev. "I could not let that happen just to cling onto power."[30]

Cuts in Soviet Defense Spending

In 1989 Gorbachev continued to antagonize his opponents in the Kremlin. He announced large cuts in military spending that raised eyebrows worldwide. He reduced the Soviet military budget by almost 15 percent and slashed production of weapons and military hardware by almost 20 percent. In a speech at the United Nations, he also pledged to remove ten thousand tanks, demobilize half a million troops, and scrap all chemical weapons. Forty thousand additional troops were withdrawn from Mongolia along the Chinese border. Many historians have seized on these cuts as proof that the US arms buildup had overwhelmed the Soviet Union. Once more, however, they are mistaken. The reductions had little to do with America's arms buildup and certainly did not represent any kind of surrender. Instead, Gorbachev urgently needed to free up resources to help his market-based reforms take hold and boost the fragile Soviet economy. As the New York Times reported, "The Soviet leader has said the top priority should be investing in new industrial technology, especially in food and other consumer goods industries to remedy the shortages that have generated widespread discontent."[31]

The idea that Reagan's arms buildup drained the Soviet economy and caused the USSR to collapse is not borne out by the facts. Even with a weakened economy, the Soviet Union had more than enough military strength to hold its republics together. North Korea and Cuba today pose two examples of Communist regimes that have maintained power by military means despite failing economies. Had Gorbachev wanted to preserve the Soviet Union at all costs, he could have done so. That he chose otherwise is what makes him such a remarkable figure in Russian history.

Chapter Four

Did Gorbachev's Reforms Make the Soviet Union's Collapse Inevitable?

Gorbachev's Reforms Could Have Preserved the Soviet Union If Pursued More Aggressively

- Unlike the hard-line members of the Politburo, Gorbachev was willing to allow the Soviet Union to become a social democracy, more like the nations of Europe.
- Glasnost and perestroika were necessary reforms that nonetheless did not go far enough to remake Soviet society.
- Maintaining authoritarian rule while reforming the Soviet economy with market-based principles could have led to increased prosperity, as in Communist China today.

The Debate at a Glance

Gorbachev's Reforms Inevitably Led to the Soviet Union's Collapse

- Gorbachev's glasnost policy was the key reform that led to the collapse of the Soviet Union.
- Beginning with the nuclear accident at Chernobyl, glasnost brought to light the failings of the Soviet government.
- The new openness in the Soviet media led to revelations about the Soviet state that brought its legitimacy into question.

Gorbachev's Reforms Could Have Preserved the Soviet Union If Pursued More Aggressively

"[The Communist Party] had become a brake on reforms even though it had launched them. But they all thought the reforms only needed to be cosmetic. They thought that painting the facade was enough, when actually there was still the same old mess inside the building."

—Former Soviet general secretary Mikhail Gorbachev, in a 2011 interview

Quoted in Jonathan Steele, "Mikhail Gorbachev: I Should Have Abandoned the Communist Party Earlier," *Guardian* (Manchester), August 16, 2011. www.theguardian.com.

Consider these questions as you read:

1. Do you believe that a more aggressive approach to reform would have saved the Soviet Union from collapse? Why or why not?
2. Was Gorbachev well suited to lead the reform movement in the Soviet Union? Explain.
3. How could Gorbachev and his deputies have persuaded the Soviet people to support his reform program?

Editor's note: The discussion that follows presents common arguments made in support of this perspective. All arguments are supported by facts, quotes, and examples taken from various sources of the period or present day.

Mikhail Gorbachev had the right idea in his attempt to reform the Soviet state. The main reason for his failure—and the collapse of the Soviet Union—lay in a program that was much too tentative for the circumstances. Gorbachev's reforms did not proceed rapidly enough or go far enough to bring about the changes that were desperately needed. In his efforts to appease hard-liners in the Kremlin, who opposed most of the reforms and urged caution, he lost the support of liberal activists and ordinary workers who demanded political and economic change to improve their everyday lives. Gorbachev learned the danger of taking halfway measures to address a full-blown crisis. In the end he even allowed his main political rival, Boris Yeltsin, to outmaneuver him and hasten the breakup of the Soviet Union.

A Society in Crisis

The task Gorbachev faced in reversing his nation's decline was a daunting one. The feeble Soviet economy had stopped growing. Central planning could not allocate resources as efficiently as market forces and individual decisions. Production of consumer goods lagged far behind the needs of the populace. Grumbling about shoddy merchandise and food shortages was widespread. People carried shopping bags to work in case they should learn about a neighborhood store receiving a small shipment of meat or vegetables during the day. When Gorbachev's reform programs failed to produce tangible change, the people felt betrayed once more. A commonly heard joke that reflected public disgust described a man who had spent hours waiting in line to buy liquor. "'I have had enough, save my place, I am going to shoot Gorbachev.' Two hours later he returns to claim his place in line. His friends ask, 'Did you get him?' 'No, the line there was even longer than the line here.'"[32]

Soviet workers had long grown accustomed to their society's depressing reality. Daily frustration led many to drink heavily. Alcoholism was a main cause of missed work and lack of productivity. Domestic abuse roiled many households. Meanwhile, Soviet apparatchiks dined in elegant, well-stocked restaurants, shopped at special government stores, and vacationed at scenic dachas, or vacation homes, located on the Black Sea. Censorship of newspapers and magazines killed stories about the true state of affairs in the Soviet Union. Books and articles by banned writers such as Aleksandr Solzhenitsyn were circulated in samizdat, which were cheap handwritten or typewritten versions. Those found with politically charged samizdat could be jailed or shipped off to the gulag, which was the state's system of political prison camps in Siberia. Despite the suppression of news, rumors about troubles in Afghanistan or the satellite nations of Eastern Europe seeped out like puffs of steam from a boiling pot. Dissatisfaction continued to build among ordinary citizens, most of whom had ceased to believe the government's official lies long ago.

Gorbachev recognized the urgent need for reform. He tackled the job with his characteristic energy and optimism. Unfortunately, he was faced with a society so stagnant and dysfunctional that it seemed resistant to change. Only a more radical approach than anything Gorbachev was willing to try had any real chance of success.

Soviet women wave their hands and shout for the few cuts of meat available from a Moscow butcher. In the early 1990s, food shortages and crises in consumer goods production intensified public dissatisfaction with the Soviet system and the slowness of change under Gorbachev.

Reforms Not Sweeping Enough

Perestroika, Gorbachev's plan to restructure the Soviet economy, stopped short of the major overhaul necessary for success. To forge a market economy, Gorbachev needed to accomplish at least three things. First, he had to establish ownership rights for individuals. Second, business and industry had to be freed from government supervision and allowed to serve their customers' needs. Third, failure had to play its part in the economic system. Firms needed the authority to fire employees, and failing enterprises had to be allowed to go bankrupt. Subsidizing unprofitable businesses had to cease.

Instead of undertaking these major reforms, Gorbachev and his fellow reformers tinkered around the edges with minor adjustments. For example, to inspire workers to be more productive, posters went up in factories and workplaces urging "intensification and acceleration"[33]—which apparently meant that more *intense* effort would produce *accelerated* growth. But this approach was nothing new. Soviet workers had been hectored with posters and slogans for decades. A more adventurous scheme might have introduced incentives for workers such as profit sharing or bonuses for better results. Chronically unproductive workers might have lost their jobs. However, such ideas clashed with the Communist focus on the collective rather than the individual. As *Pravda*, the Soviet daily newspaper, put it, "The Party will continue to wage a very resolute struggle against all negative phenomena alien to the socialist way of life and to our communist morality."[34] Thus, a person's job was considered permanent, which fostered security but also left little enthusiasm for improving job skills. Party dogma continued to outweigh economic performance.

> "The Party will continue to wage a very resolute struggle against all negative phenomena alien to the socialist way of life and to our communist morality."[34]
>
> —An editorial in *Pravda*, the Soviet Communist Party's daily newspaper

Elsewhere, certain hopelessly backward factories and businesses were allowed to close, but only a limited number of privately owned enterprises opened to take their place. When these businesses sold goods for prices four or five times the government's subsidized price, citizens howled about profiteering. In 1990 a Moscow McDonald's restaurant appeared, the first of its kind in the nation, although few Soviet citizens could afford to sample a hamburger. Interested farmers could apply to lease land for agriculture, but outright ownership was still forbidden. Those who obtained farm leases faced terrible problems with infrastructure. Roads from farm to market were inadequate, when they existed at all; facilities for crop storage and refrigeration were lacking; and credit for new farm businesses was not a priority. Each failure of an independent farm or enterprise served Gorbachev's opponents in the Communist Party as evidence against what they considered to be his reckless reforms.

Party Betrayal

Ultimately, Gorbachev's reform program was betrayed by powerful forces behind the scenes in the Communist Party. As Gorbachev noted, party hard-liners in the Kremlin supported the appearance of reform but not the fundamental changes necessary to make it work. Members of the old guard, accustomed to the perks of their lofty positions, were not going to give them up without a fight. Gorbachev decided that the Communist Party had to be stripped of its monopoly on political power. This was the only way he would be able to implement his economic plan. With glasnost, he doubled down on free speech and open inquiry into the brutal reign of Stalin and other Soviet leaders. Stories about corruption and political favors filled the media. In 1989 Gorbachev made good on his promises of democratic reforms. Elections were held throughout the Soviet Union, with most winning candidates running in opposition to the Communist line. Many attacked Gorbachev himself as an incompetent leader. He acknowledged the messiness of the process but felt it was a healthy first step. "The lineup of candidates was worthy, although there were some who acted for personal gain," Gorbachev says. "This was more evident in the capitals than anywhere else. Some candidates used all the methods of cheek, impudence, demagoguery, and irresponsible promises. And they won that way."[35]

Nonetheless, much as he hoped the Soviet Union would eventually become a social democracy like the governments of Western Europe, Gorbachev stopped short of dissolving the Communist Party. He refused to disavow Marxism-Leninism completely. Marxism was the radical socialist philosophy of the German Karl Marx on which the Soviet Union's system of government was based. Leninism was Vladimir Lenin's version of Marxism, which set up a one-party Communist dictatorship controlled by revolutionaries. This attempt to have things both ways would be Gorbachev's undoing. In 1991, with events spinning out of control, hard-liners in the Communist Party captured Gorbachev and his wife in an attempted coup. By failing to root out his enemies in the Kremlin—as well as his main political rival, the anti-Communist Yeltsin—Gorbachev found himself on the sidelines as the Soviet Union collapsed. One year later Gorbachev lost to Yeltsin in the election for president of Russia by a landslide. His failed reforms had made him a pariah among his own people.

The Chinese Example

On May 17, 1989, Mikhail Gorbachev had delivered a speech in China's capital of Beijing. In the speech, he explained his rationale for granting his nation's first contested elections in decades: "Economic reform will not work unless supported by a radical transformation of the political system."[36] Deng Xiaoping, the leader of China's Communist Party, believed just the opposite. He pursued the goal of a market economy while clamping down on political speech. As Deng's youngest son reported, "My father thinks Gorbachev is an idiot."[37] One month after Gorbachev's visit, Deng sent troops to break up pro-democracy demonstrations in Tiananmen Square.

> "Economic reform will not work unless supported by a radical transformation of the political system."[36]
>
> —Mikhail Gorbachev, in a May 17, 1989, speech in Beijing, China

Hundreds of protesters, perhaps many more, were murdered. Yet Deng and the Chinese Communist Party held on to power and transformed China into an economic powerhouse, albeit one with a harshly authoritarian government. Gorbachev could have used force to hold the Soviet Union together, but he refused. For him, a statesman whose reforms in many ways did not go far enough, it was a step much too far.

Gorbachev's Reforms Inevitably Led to the Soviet Union's Collapse

"[Chernobyl] was a catalyst for glasnost, the opening-up of the Soviet media, which exposed the flaws of the Soviet system and set off the chain reaction that led to its ultimate destruction."

—The *Economist*, a British journal on politics and economics

Economist, "A Nuclear Disaster That Brought Down an Empire," April 26, 2016. www.economist .com.

Consider these questions as you read:

1. Do you believe glasnost was necessary? Should Gorbachev have focused only on economic reform? Explain.
2. How important was the Chernobyl nuclear disaster in establishing glasnost reforms in the Soviet Union? Explain.
3. Do you agree that Gorbachev's reform efforts were doomed to failure from the start? Why or why not?

Editor's note: The discussion that follows presents common arguments made in support of this perspective. All arguments are supported by facts, quotes, and examples taken from various sources of the period or present day.

Most histories blame the Soviet Union's demise on its sagging economy and the failure of Mikhail Gorbachev's perestroika reforms to make needed improvements. But the more crucial reform was glasnost—Gorbachev's policy of free speech and open exchange of information. Glasnost affected the Soviet Union like a poison pill that made the collapse inevitable. Or perhaps it was more like a flood of sunlight, revealing all the rot and corruption that had accumulated in the seventy years since the October Revolution had ushered in the country's Communist system.

Before glasnost, Soviet citizens read stories in *Pravda* like coded messages, trying to infer the kernel of truth buried in the propaganda. Dispatches about the Soviet economy stressed the great strides being made in manufacturing and steel production. Soviet collective farms were portrayed as oases of roaming live-stock and rich produce. News about the United States and other Western nations emphasized racial tensions, poverty, and exploi-tation of workers. Gorbachev himself admits to this strategy of deceit. "We, including I, were saying, 'Capitalism is moving to-ward a catastrophe, whereas we are developing well,'" he says. "Of course, that was pure propaganda. In fact, our country was lagging behind."[38]

Told repeatedly they were living in a workers' paradise, So-viet citizens too often found empty shelves when they went to buy meat, vegetables, toothpaste, detergent, or pantyhose. Fear of being overheard by the wrong people kept them silent about the real state of affairs. Everyone basically knew the truth, but no one was willing to speak. This created an enormous pressurized bubble of pent-up anger and frustration. And glasnost was the pin that burst the bubble.

A Test of Glasnost

An early test of glasnost dealt with the deadly accident at the Chernobyl nuclear power plant, which occurred on April 26, 1986. At first Soviet propaganda held sway as in the past. While firefighters battled the blaze, receiving lethal doses of radiation, Soviet officials remained silent. Only when sensors located in Sweden detected high levels of radioactivity did the Soviets ad-mit to the accident. As stories about Chernobyl flooded the world press, the Moscow News, a propaganda newspaper, claimed it was all a premeditated anti-Soviet campaign cooked up by the United States and NATO.

Gorbachev reacted with fury at how information was being with-held not only from the public but from him and other members of the Central Committee, the ruling body of delegates that made de-cisions for the Communist Party. He realized that he and his reform

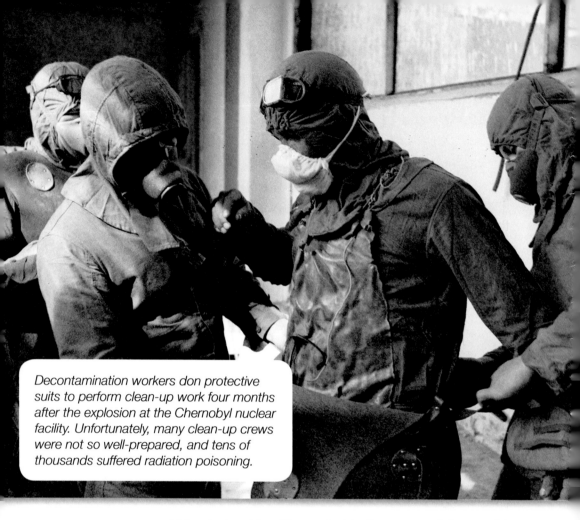

Decontamination workers don protective suits to perform clean-up work four months after the explosion at the Chernobyl nuclear facility. Unfortunately, many clean-up crews were not so well-prepared, and tens of thousands suffered radiation poisoning.

program would be judged by Chernobyl in the eyes of the world. Gorbachev appointed a new editor dedicated to free speech to head the illustrated weekly *Ogonyok*, which had a readership of 1.5 million. The *Moscow News* abandoned Cold War propaganda for reliable reports about Gorbachev's reforms. "These publications, and others that followed suit, undermined one of the main pillars of the Soviet system: its ability to lie," wrote the *Economist*. "Five years after the explosion at Chernobyl, that inability to conceal the truth would bring down the whole rotten construction."[39]

A Moral Crusade

Glasnost was essentially a moral crusade. Before the economy could be revamped and strengthened, before Soviet society could be revitalized, the nation had to face its moral failings over many years. Gorbachev's policy of openness was aimed at bringing about a reappraisal of core values in Soviet society. He and his few staunch supporters in the Kremlin viewed the Soviet system as corrupt and spiritually empty. To turn things around, they insisted, it was necessary to examine the past in detail and openly admit where Soviet leaders had used criminal tactics to maintain power and oppress the people. Ordinary citizens also had to be held to account. Laziness, dishonesty, physical abuse, thievery, drunkenness—they had all contributed to social decline. At the January 1987 meeting of the Central Committee in which Gorbachev announced his policies of glasnost and democratization, he declared, "A new moral atmosphere is taking shape in the country."[40] Nikolai Ryzhkov, Gorbachev's prime minister, blasted the corruption and lies at the heart of Soviet society: "We stole from ourselves, took and gave bribes, lied in the reports, in newspapers, from high podiums, wallowed in our lies, hung medals on one another. And all of this—from top to bottom and from bottom to top."[41]

In unmasking the past, Gorbachev had an example to follow. In the early 1950s, after the death of Joseph Stalin, Soviet leader Nikita Khrushchev had shocked the Politburo with a remarkably candid speech addressing Stalin's crimes. Previously unmentionable, these crimes included the Great Terror of the 1930s, a campaign in which Stalin had ordered the murders of hundreds of thousands of loyal Communist Party members simply to sow fear and ensure the loyalty of those who survived. Under glasnost Gorbachev outdid Khrushchev. Party archives were thrown open to historians.

> "We stole from ourselves, took and gave bribes, lied in the reports, in newspapers, from high podiums, wallowed in our lies, hung medals on one another. And all of this—from top to bottom and from bottom to top."[41]
>
> —Nikolai Ryzhkov, Gorbachev's prime minister, commenting on Soviet society

Scholars were able to analyze Stalin's murderous legacy in great detail (although Vladimir Lenin, whose own bloody directives were kept secret for several more years, remained a sainted hero of the October Revolution). As books and articles rolled out, filled with debunked myths and grim revelations about the Communist Party, people began to feel as if the ground was shifting under their feet. Long-held views about the virtues of communism went up in smoke.

The Truth About the Economy

Freed from government censorship, Soviet journalists began to report honestly on the economy. *Komsomolskaya Pravda*, the youth newspaper of the Communist Party, pointed out that whereas Russia had ranked seventh in the world in per capita consumption (the value of goods and services consumed by individuals on average) before the 1917 revolution, by the late 1980s it had fallen to seventy-seventh. Ideals of universal equality were shown up as a sham. Government failures were blamed for widespread poverty. Economists estimated that 45 percent of the Soviet Union's 285 million citizens lived below the poverty line. Only about 11 percent could be considered middle class or well off. Newspaper stories examined the shoddy conditions most Soviet citizens had to endure. *Washington Post* correspondent David Remnick notes the truths about everyday life that glasnost uncovered:

> There was the sheer crumminess of the things that you could find: the plastic shoes, the sulfurous mineral water, the collapsible apartment buildings. The decrepitude of ordinary life irritated the soul and skin. Towels scratched after one washing, milk soured in a day, cars collapsed upon purchase. The leading cause of house fires in the Soviet Union was television sets that exploded spontaneously. All of it kept people in a constant state of frustration and misery. Glasnost meant admitting to all this, too.[42]

Russian black humor produced backhanded tributes to Soviet consumer goods. In a large exhibition hall in Moscow, the USSR Consumer Society joined with a weekly tabloid to set up the Exhibit of Poor Quality Goods. The collection included blouses with split seams, chipped bowls, rusted teapots, oblong volleyballs, spoiled lettuce, and a bottle of water with a tiny dead mouse inside. Visitors flocked to the show, although many had to admit it was no worse than their local market. Marina Nitchkina, a Soviet specialist in quality control, explains:

> "There was the sheer crumminess of the things that you could find: the plastic shoes, the sulfurous mineral water, the collapsible apartment buildings. . . . All of it kept people in a constant state of frustration and misery. Glasnost meant admitting to all this, too."[42]
>
> —*Washington Post* correspondent David Remnick

Part of the problem is that for years the economic planners thought only about quantity—pumping out the merchandise, the steel or whatever—but they had no conception of what quality meant. Part of the pleasant, though painful, effect of glasnost is that more and more people are seeing, or even buying, Western products and understanding the huge difference. And they are demanding that Soviet products be just as good.[43]

Loss of Legitimacy

If the Soviet Union failed miserably at distribution of goods, glasnost proved a huge success at distributing knowledge. With controls loosened for radio, television, the press, and the film industry, the Soviet public received a daily dose of truth telling. Inevitably, public opinion became impossible for Gorbachev and his deputies to manage. If all Soviet institutions were fair game for scrutiny, then he and the Communist Party also had to pay the price. The grand Soviet project of Socialist engineering on a massive scale, a project for which so many had sacrificed their freedom and their lives, stood revealed as a muddled failure. As a result, the regime lost legitimacy in the minds of citizens from Russia to Armenia and from Moldova to Tajikistan. Beginning with the Baltic States, the various republics broke away from the USSR. They held their own elections and pursued their own destinies. Gorbachev once declared, "I detest lies."[44] Allowing the truth to emerge about the Soviet Union proved to be its undoing.

Chapter Five

Is Today's Russia More or Less of a Threat than the Soviet Union Was?

Today's Russia Is a Greater Threat to the West than the Soviet Union Was

- Vladimir Putin, the president of Russia, is a former KGB officer who runs the country like a mob boss determined to intimidate his foes.
- Putin has resorted to assassination of political enemies and journalists as well as invasions of Georgia and Ukraine.
- Putin is determined to spread Russian influence in the Middle East and Europe by any means necessary.

The Debate at a Glance

Today's Russia Is Less of a Threat to the West than the Soviet Union Was

- With the collapse of the Soviet Union and the end of the Warsaw Pact, Putin as ruler of Russia has much fewer resources under his control.
- The Soviet Union was determined to spread Communist regimes throughout the world, while Putin has no ideological goals.
- China has replaced the Soviet Union as the West's main adversary in the world.

Today's Russia Is a Greater Threat to the West than the Soviet Union Was

"All the life of Russia is subordinate to the realization of its new global foreign policy goal: to frighten the West and force it to retreat, lift sanctions, and open the capital market for the regime."

—Vladimir Pastukhov, historian at the London School of Economics

Quoted in Paul A. Goble, "Anti-Americanism Is 'Cult of Putin's Russia' with All the Consequences Thereof, Pastukhov Says," *Euromaidan Press*, October 15, 2016. http://euromaidanpress.com.

Consider these questions as you read:

1. Do you agree that Russia today poses a greater threat to the West than the Soviet Union did? Why or why not?
2. Should the United States continue trying to work with Vladimir Putin in resolving world crises? Explain.
3. What could the United States do to reduce the threat from Russia?

Editor's note: The discussion that follows presents common arguments made in support of this perspective. All arguments are supported by facts, quotes, and examples taken from various sources of the period or present day.

When the Soviet Union collapsed in 1991, the United States, and the West in general, seemed to have won a major victory. Communism had succumbed to liberal democracy and free markets. Even the Communist leadership in China was pursuing economic change. Large-scale wars and global tensions based on ideological clashes seemed thankfully a thing of the past. In a celebrated 1992 essay, the American political scientist Francis Fukuyama actually proclaimed the end of history: "What we are witnessing is not just the end of the Cold War, or a passing of a particular period of post-war history, but the end of history as such: that is, the end point of mankind's ideological evolution and the universalization of Western liberal democracy as the final form of human government."[45]

Russia, as opposed to the Soviet Union, presented no particular threat to the West—or so ran the conventional wisdom. President Barack Obama and members of his administration sought ways to work with Vladimir Putin, the former KGB agent who has ruled Russia for years with an iron will and cunning. Early in Obama's presidency, Secretary of State Hillary Clinton declared a so-called reset with Russia that supposedly would lead to closer relations. In 2012 Obama mocked his presidential opponent Mitt Romney for warning that Russia remained America's chief foreign adversary. "The 1980s are now calling to ask for their foreign policy back," Obama said, "because the Cold War's been over for 20 years."[46]

Today all that has changed. Far from becoming a trusted partner with the United States, Putin's Russia has become its most lethal enemy. From his military forays to support dictator Bashar

The administration of US President Barack Obama sought ways to work with the new Soviet Union, which arose in the decades after the Cold War and glasnost. However, Russian President Vladimir Putin proved to be a cagey and combative adversary rather than a trusted partner.

al-Assad in Syria to his attempts to reclaim Georgia, Ukraine, and Crimea by force, Putin has shown his disdain for American interests. He has stationed nuclear missiles along the borders of Lithuania and Poland. Russian fighter jets have buzzed NATO aircraft over the Baltic Sea. In response to US sanctions, Putin ejected hundreds of American diplomats and embassy personnel and let it be known that relations would not improve anytime soon. Meanwhile, to spur national pride, he resorted to the traditional tactics of Soviet leaders—overseeing a naval parade of Russian warships and submarines in Saint Petersburg. Russian computer hackers have been accused of meddling in the 2016 US presidential election, a charge that Putin blandly calls a lie. Such antics would have been considered a major provocation during the Cold War, but Putin seems to enjoy ratcheting up the tension. The thought of a wrong step leading to a nuclear conflict does not deter him from seeking every advantage. It is this heedless quality that makes Putin's Russia a more dangerous threat to the West than the Soviet Union ever was.

Soviet Collapse a Disaster

A major reason for Putin's belligerence is what he considers the humiliation of the Soviet Union's breakup. In a 2005 speech in Moscow, Putin left no doubt about his own view of the collapse: "First and foremost it is worth acknowledging that the demise of the Soviet Union was the greatest geopolitical catastrophe of the century. As for the Russian people, it became a genuine tragedy. Tens of millions of our fellow citizens and countrymen found themselves beyond the fringes of Russian territory. The epidemic of collapse has spilled over to Russia itself."[47]

Although he avoids public criticism of Mikhail Gorbachev, Putin no doubt blames him for the collapse and reckons his failed reform program a huge blunder. Putin seems determined not to make the same mistakes. He has mouthed support for democracy while ruthlessly eliminating any challenge to his rule. He prefers the most brazen acts to assert his dominance. Opponents of his regime who attain a high profile tend to die violently. Journalist and human rights activist Anna Politkovskaya was murdered in the elevator of her apartment building. Alexander Litvinenko, a former secret service officer who specialized in rooting out organized crime, lost his life to radiation poisoning from a spiked cup of tea he drank in a London hotel. Attorney Sergei Magnitsky, who had uncovered possible long-term state-sanctioned theft, expired in police custody after a brutal beating. Boris Nemtsov, a physicist and liberal politician who became one of Putin's fiercest critics, died from a gunshot wound on a bridge just outside the Kremlin. Although Putin denies any connection to these events, such tactics hark back to the Communist Party's bloody purges of the 1930s and, many believe, mark Putin as a deadly successor to Joseph Stalin. He operates much like a mob boss, enriching certain cronies to keep them in line and cutting off others who stray from the fold.

All the while Putin dreams of restoring Russia to what he regards as its former Soviet-era glory. When the Soviet Union fell, he was a KGB agent stationed in East Germany. He seethed with resentment as Gorbachev refused to crack down on protests in Eastern Europe that led to the USSR's downfall. Today that anger and resentment helps fuel his aggressive foreign policy. With no one inside Russia to push back against his whims, Putin can indulge in brinkmanship all he wants. "A weak, insecure, unpredictable country with nuclear weapons is dangerous—more so, in some ways, even than the Soviet Union was," says an editorial in the *Economist*. "Unlike Soviet leaders after Stalin, Mr. Putin rules alone, unchecked by a Politburo or by having witnessed the second world war's devastation. He could remain in charge for years to come. Age is unlikely to mellow him."[48]

> "A weak, insecure, unpredictable country with nuclear weapons is dangerous—more so, in some ways, even than the Soviet Union was. Unlike Soviet leaders after Stalin, Mr. Putin rules alone, unchecked by a Politburo."[48]
>
> —An editorial in the *Economist*, a British news and opinion publication

A Dangerous Quest for Respect

One word that jumps out in assessing Russia today is *insecurity*. Putin is desperately seeking respect for Russia as a major power, despite its sagging economy and dysfunctional form of government. Like the Soviet leaders Joseph Stalin and Nikita Khrushchev at the height of the Cold War, he knows that he cannot compete with the West on even terms, so he blusters and acts aggressively. Any perceived slight from the United States or other Western nations can trigger the tyrant's paranoia. The danger is that Putin and his generals will take some rash action in an attempt to assert Russia's importance on the world stage. As Russian political writer Arkady Ostrovsky notes:

> "It's a dangerous situation. It comes down to the game of chicken, like in any deterrence. Putin believes that the West will always blink first; he needs to be dissuaded of that notion."[49]
>
> —Russian political writer Arkady Ostrovsky

The key point is that Russia is acting like this out of weakness and insecurity, rather than strength and confidence. . . . Given Putin's willingness to use military power for political goals and his threats to use nuclear weapons, I think you have to engage in a conversation with Putin, by the same logic you would engage in a conversation with a terrorist who's holding hostages and is threatening to blow them up. . . . It's a dangerous situation. It comes down to the game of chicken, like in any deterrence. Putin believes that the West will always blink first; he needs to be dissuaded of that notion.[49]

Like the Soviet Union, Putin's Russia needs enemies to justify itself and rally its people. Putin deflects attention from the murders of his political opponents and his own authoritarian rule by playing on Russian fears about the United States and the outside world. And it is important to remember that Russia today is a nation in which almost half the people approve of the brutal dictator Stalin. Putin knows that a leader who aggressively stands up to foreign adversaries can maintain support at home. Thus, although he has failed to solve Russia's long-term problems of economic growth and inequality, his popularity mostly remains intact. "Indeed, he and his cronies have compounded [these problems] with their own misgovernment," says Theodore R. Bromund, senior research fellow at the Heritage Foundation. "When Putin's hack mouthpiece, *Russia Today*, names 'corruption' as one of the key threats facing Russia, you have to laugh. Yes, corruption [is] endemic in Russia. But the most corrupt people in Russia sit in the Kremlin."[50] And ousting them anytime soon seems unlikely.

During the Cold War many security experts in the West viewed the Soviet Union as virtually a Third World nation with a First World nuclear arsenal. In Russia today that gap is even more pronounced. Russia's nuclear missiles transform Putin from a regional bully into a serious threat to world peace—a threat even greater than the Soviet Union presented.

Today's Russia Is Less of a Threat to the West than the Soviet Union Was

"Russia does not pose the challenge the Soviet Union once did. It is a smaller, weaker power."

—Eugene Rumer, director and senior fellow at the Carnegie Endowment for International Peace

Eugene Rumer, "Russia—a Different Kind of Threat," Carnegie Endowment for International Peace, July 20, 2015. http://carnegieendowment.org.

Consider these questions as you read:

1. What characteristics made the Soviet Union a more dangerous threat than Russia today? Could these things have been changed with reform?
2. Why do you think many experts downplay the threat that the Soviet Union presented to the West?
3. Do you believe ideology makes a nation a more dangerous enemy overall? Explain.

Editor's note: The discussion that follows presents common arguments made in support of this perspective. All arguments are supported by facts, quotes, and examples taken from various sources of the period or present day.

A strange reversal has taken place among the sophisticates who comment on foreign policy in the United States. The same experts who once rolled their eyes at Ronald Reagan's anticommunism and insisted that Cold War fears about the Soviet Union were ridiculously overblown now see Russia as a much greater threat. Sad to say, these not-so-sober thinkers are wrong on both counts. Despite Vladimir Putin's devious plots and numerous offenses against liberal values, today's Russia presents nothing like the Soviet Union's threat to the West at the height of the Cold War. Certainly, Putin's thuggish rule offends lovers of freedom, but he is scarcely worse than any number of other authoritarians in the world, from central Asia to the Middle East to northern Africa. He is by no means a second Stalin. Even Putin's supposed meddling in foreign elections, including the 2016 US presidential race, is more likely an attempt to sow discord, not change outcomes. When the Soviets chose to influence political events, they would send in a column of tanks and put a stop to liberal reforms, as in Hungary in 1956 and Czechoslovakia in 1968.

One key difference between Putin's Russia and the Soviet Union is ideology. Putin cares nothing for Communist revolution or ideology of any kind. By contrast, the Soviets thrived on it. For them, Marxist-Leninist doctrine colored every aspect of political life. As the Nobel Prize–winning writer Aleksandr Solzhenitsyn observed in *The Gulag Archipelago*, his exposé of the Soviet prison camp system, "Thanks to ideology, the twentieth century was fated to experience evildoing on a scale of millions."[51] The breakup of the Soviet Union meant the West had triumphed over Communist ideology, at least in its Russian form. Putin may regret the collapse and loss of empire, but his Russia no longer seeks wider conquests. Doug Bandow, former special assistant to President Ronald Reagan, explains:

> "Russia today is not engaged in a global ideological battle with America. However cynical the old Communist leadership, the Soviet Union posed an ideological and moral challenge to the U.S."[52]
>
> —Doug Bandow, former special assistant to President Ronald Reagan

Russia today is not engaged in a global ideological battle with America. However cynical the old Communist leadership, the Soviet Union posed an ideological and moral challenge to the U.S. Many people around the world were attracted to Communism for a time, at least, and even some Americans thought they saw the future at work. . . . The Russian remnant of Ronald Reagan's Evil Empire is no philosophical heir to the U.S.S.R. Moscow offers no alternative ideology with appeal around the globe. . . . Russian money may have rented some activists, politicians, and parties in Europe, but ultimately they will rise or fall on their own.[52]

Fewer Resources for War

Another reason Russia poses much less of a threat than the Soviet Union is lack of military resources. Whereas Putin retains the nuclear arsenal of his Soviet forebears, Russia's military strength overall has declined since the end of the Cold War. The sort of full-scale invasion launched by the Soviets in Afghanistan in 1979 lies well beyond Russia's capabilities today. It is important to remember that the Soviet Union could call on resources from its

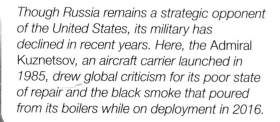

Though Russia remains a strategic opponent of the United States, its military has declined in recent years. Here, the Admiral Kuznetsov, *an aircraft carrier launched in 1985, drew global criticism for its poor state of repair and the black smoke that poured from its boilers while on deployment in 2016.*

non-Russian republics plus the other nations in the Warsaw Pact, the Soviet military alliance. Putin has invested in advanced missile systems and spent large sums to modernize the Russian military, but it still lags behind Soviet levels. When the *Admiral Kuznetsov*, an antiquated Russian aircraft carrier, deployed to the Syrian conflict recently, it drew notice not for its size or speed but for the thick black smoke it was belching. "It is expected back in dry dock after the Syria deployment because its propulsion system needs to be replaced," reported Neil MacFarquhar in the *New York Times*. "Whenever it went to sea over the years, the *Admiral Kuznetsov* was prone to accidents."[53]

As with the Soviet Union, much of Russian wealth today is tied to the value of commodities such as oil, natural gas, coal, and raw aluminum. The recent drop in oil prices has reduced profits from Gazprom, Russia's state-owned energy company, leaving less room in the budget for military spending. US sanctions for Putin's incursions in Crimea and Ukraine have added to Russian economic woes. One expert estimated that the value of the ruble has been cut in half, while Russia's GDP has fallen by as much as 35 percent. Putin's flexing of military muscle in Syria and elsewhere may be an attempt to divert attention from his nation's struggling economy. And while it's true that a wounded bear may be especially dangerous, Russia under Putin does not pose the same threat to the world that the Soviet Union once did.

No Longer America's Chief Adversary

During the Cold War there was no doubt that the Soviet Union was America's main opponent. Every foreign policy question took into account the Soviet drive for power and influence. Cold War strategists on both sides sought advantages across the globe, like grand masters moving pieces on a chessboard. The Soviets, alarmed by anti-Communist rhetoric from President John F. Kennedy in the early 1960s, made contingency plans to invade Western Europe with Warsaw Pact troops should the right opportunity arise. The Kremlin even considered the use of nuclear weapons along with conventional forces. But this level of threat vanished with the collapse of the Soviet Union. Swayed by Putin's headline-grabbing stunts, many observers lazily assume that Russia once more looms as America's deadliest threat. But in reality the United States and the West face challenges elsewhere in the world that are just as urgent.

In fact, America's chief adversary now is not Russia but China. Unlike the Communist Party of the Soviet Union in its waning days, the Chinese Communist Party has never flinched from hard measures in maintaining its grip on power. Even when Deng Xiaoping chucked the party's five-year plans for market-based reforms—called socialism with Chinese characteristics—he still cracked down on pro-democracy forces. Gigantic images of Chairman Mao Zedong, the founder of the Chinese Communist Party, continue to appear in public squares. Open debate is hobbled by censorship. Current president Xi Jinping has stressed repeatedly his devotion to communism and strict party rule. China's remarkable growth has also produced ambitions to challenge the West. According to historian Ian Buruma, "China plainly aspires to be the dominant power in East and Southeast Asia, and this is making the United States and its allies increasingly nervous."[54] Ironically, the Chinese threat, much more than that of Putin's Russia, resembles America's Cold War competition with a committed ideological foe—only this time the opponent has a strong economy, a subdued populace, and endless patience.

The Ideological Component

In the end it was the ideological component that made the Soviet Union a much more dangerous enemy than Russia today. Putin's efforts to boost his nation's profile in the world bear the usual stamp of power politics. He measures his success by wealth and influence. But the Soviet Union was founded on a utopian goal: to create a worker's paradise where everyone shares equally in society's benefits. This idea led to fanaticism on the part of Vladimir Lenin and those dedicated Communists who came after him. If the ultimate goal is considered to be righteous beyond question, then anything done to achieve that goal is justified. This thought process, as it played out in the seventy years of Soviet rule, led to mass imprisonment of so-called enemies of the people in Siberian prison camps, murderous purges and forced famines to secure the party's aims, and oppressive rule that left the people cringing in poverty, fear, and paranoia. It was Soviet ideology that prompted Nikita Khrushchev to warn the West, "We will bury you!"[55] That ideology also produced tens of millions of victims in the quest for utopia.

> "[The Soviet Union] was not a good idea that somehow went wrong or withered away. It was a very bad idea from the outset."[56]
>
> —British novelist Martin Amis

The year 2017 marked the hundredth anniversary of the Russian Revolution. Books, articles, and editorials debated Soviet history and the final collapse. More than a few experts, while admitting the unfortunate details, saw the Soviet Union as a grand experiment. Others, such as British novelist Martin Amis, condemned the whole enterprise. "It was not a good idea that somehow went wrong or withered away," wrote Amis. "It was a very bad idea from the outset. . . . The chief demerit of the Marxist program was its point-by-point defiance of human nature."[56] Such a regime made for a more dangerous enemy than many are willing to admit—an enemy that was a far greater threat than the country that emerged from its collapse.

Source Notes

Chapter One: A Brief History of the Soviet Union's Collapse

1. Quoted in Marc Bennetts, "25th Anniversary of Soviet Coup Met with Hostility, Indifference in Russia," *Washington Times*, August 21, 2016. www.washingtontimes.com.
2. Robert F. Baumann, "Compound War Case Study: The Soviets in Afghanistan," GlobalSecurity.org, September 19, 2001. www.globalsecurity.org.
3. Ronald Reagan, "Evil Empire Speech," March 8, 1983. www.nationalcenter.org.
4. Quoted in Heritage Foundation, "20 Years Later: Reagan's Westminster Speech: June 8, 1982," June 4, 2002. www.heritage.org.
5. Quoted in William R. Hawkins, "How SDI Pushed the USSR into the Abyss," Selous Foundation for Public Policy Research, September 21, 2014. http://sfppr.org.
6. Quoted in Rodric Braithwaite, "Fall of the Berlin Wall: The Iron Curtain Fell Because of Mikhail Gorbachev—Yet Today He Is Despised as a Traitor by Russians," *Independent* (London), November 9, 2014. www.independent.co.uk.
7. Quoted in Brigid McCarthy, "Gorbachev, Yeltsin and the Demise of the USSR," PRI, September 26, 2011. www.pri.org.

Chapter Two: Was the Soviet Invasion of Afghanistan a Key Factor in the Soviet Union's Collapse?

8. Rupert Colley, "Hafizullah Amin—a Summary," History in an Hour, August 1, 2012. www.historyinanhour.com.
9. Robert Wilde, "The Brezhnev Doctrine," ThoughtCo., August 31, 2017. www.thoughtco.com.
10. Directorate of Intelligence, "The Costs of Soviet Involvement in Afghanistan: An Intelligence Assessment," Central Intelligence Agency, February 1987. www.cia.gov.
11. Leon Aron, "Everything You Think You Know About the Collapse of the Soviet Union Is Wrong," *Foreign Policy*, June 20, 2011. http://foreignpolicy.com.

12. Jonathan Steele, "10 Myths About Afghanistan," *Guardian* (Manchester), September 27, 2011. www.theguardian.com.

13. J. Bruce Amstutz, *Afghanistan: The First Five Years of Soviet Occupation*. Honolulu: University Press of the Pacific, 2002, p. 158.

14. Patrick Cockburn, "The Russians Did Better . . . So Why Did They Lose?," *CounterPunch*, December 8, 2010. www.counter punch.org.

15. Quoted in Alexander Lyakhovsky, "Afghanistan and the Soviet Withdrawal 1989— 20 Years Later," National Security Archive, February 15, 2009. http://nsarchive2.gwu.edu.

16. Anil Cicek, "The Quicksand of Afghanistan: The Impact of the Afghanistan War on the Breakup of the Soviet Union," *International Journal of Russian Studies*, July 25, 2015. www .ijors.net.

17. Rafael Reuveny and Aseem Prakash, "The Afghanistan War and the Breakdown of the Soviet Union," *Review of International Studies*, 1999. https://faculty.washington.edu.

18. Quoted in Reuveny and Prakash, "The Afghanistan War and the Breakdown of the Soviet Union."

Chapter Three: Did the Arms Race Cause the Soviet Union's Collapse?

19. Quoted in Samuel Sheetz, "'We Win; They Lose': The Staggering Simplicity of Reagan's Grand Strategy," Daily Signal, December 10, 2011. http://dailysignal.com.

20. Zachary Keck, "Russia's Cold War Master Plan to Massacre NATO (and Completely Destroy Europe)," *National Interest*, January 31, 2017. http://nationalinterest.org.

21. Quoted in American Presidency Project, "Ronald Reagan: The President's News Conference, January 29, 1981." www .presidency.ucsb.edu.

22. Richard Ned Lebow and Janice Gross Stein, "Reagan and the Russians," *Atlantic*, February 1994. www.theatlantic.com.

23. Quoted in *Wall Street Journal*, "The Godfather of Missile Defense," September 5, 2017. www.wsj.com.

24. Quoted in Heritage Foundation, "20 Years Later."

25. Quoted in Strobe Talbott, Review of *Reagan and Gorbachev: Shutting the Cold War Down* by Jack F. Matlock Jr., Brookings, August 1, 2004. www.brookings.edu.

26. Talbott, Review.

27. Rozanne Ridgway, "'The Cold War Was Truly Over'—the 1986 Reykjavik Summit," Association for Diplomatic Studies and Training. http://adst.org.

28. Bruce Parrott, "The Politics of Soviet National Security Under Gorbachev," National Council for Soviet and East European Research, September 1988. www.ucis.pitt.edu.

29. Parrott, "The Politics of Soviet National Security Under Gorbachev."

30. Quoted in Damien Sharkov, "Mikhail Gorbachev on the Soviet Union Collapse, Democracy in Russia and Putin's Popularity," *Newsweek*, December 13, 2016. www.newsweek.com.

31. Bill Keller, "Gorbachev Promises Big Cut in Military Spending," *New York Times*, January 19, 1989. www.nytimes.com.

Chapter Four: Did Gorbachev's Reforms Make the Soviet Union's Collapse Inevitable?

32. Quoted in RT, "Jokes in Docs: CIA Throws in Some Laughs About Soviet Leadership in Published Papers," January 20, 2017. www.rt.com.

33. Quoted in James Graham, "Perestroika and the Soviet Economy," On This Day. www.onthisday.com.

34. Quoted in Seventeen Moments in Soviet History, "Gorbachev Proposes Restructuring." http://soviethistory.msu.edu.

35. Quoted in National Security Archive, "Transcript of CC CPSU Politburo Session, 'Outcome of the USSR People's Deputies Elections,' March 28, 1989." http://nsarchive2.gwu.edu.

36. Quoted in Chris Miller, "Could Mikhail Gorbachev Have Saved the Soviet Union?," *Foreign Policy*, December 21, 2016. http://foreignpolicy.com.

37. Quoted in Miller, "Could Mikhail Gorbachev Have Saved the Soviet Union?"

38. Quoted in Verena Dobnik, "Mikhail Gorbachev: Communism Was 'Pure Propaganda,'" Ars Technica, March 11, 2002. https://arstechnica.com.

39. *Economist*, "A Nuclear Disaster That Brought Down an Empire," April 26, 2016. www.economist.com.

40. Quoted in Aron, "Everything You Think You Know About the Collapse of the Soviet Union Is Wrong."

41. Quoted in Aron, "Everything You Think You Know About the Collapse of the Soviet Union Is Wrong."

42. David Remnick, *Lenin's Tomb: The Last Days of the Soviet Empire*. New York: Random House, 1993, p. 203.

43. Quoted in David Remnick, "Meanwhile, Soviets View a Hit Parade of Shoddy Goods," *Washington Post*, December 4, 1989. www.washingtonpost.com.

44. Quoted in Nick Anderson, "Mikhail Gorbachev," Cold War Museum, 2010. www.coldwar.org.

Chapter Five: Is Today's Russia More or Less of a Threat than the Soviet Union Was?

45. Quoted in Roger Kimball, "Francis Fukuyama and the End of History," *New Criterion*, February 1992. www.newcriterion.com.

46. Quoted in Arthur Delaney, "Obama Dings Romney on Russia Remark: The 1980s Are Calling to Ask for Their Foreign Policy Back," *Huffington Post*, October 22, 2012. www.huffington post.com.

47. Quoted in Associated Press, "Putin: Soviet Collapse a 'Tragedy,'" Fox News, April 25, 2005. www.foxnews.com.

48. *Economist*, "The Threat from Russia," October 22, 2016. www.economist.com.

49. Peter Pomerantsev and Arkady Ostrovsky, "What Vladimir Putin Wants from America's Elections," *Atlantic*, November 6, 2016. www.theatlantic.com.

50. Theodore R. Bromund, "Russia's Insecurity Strategy," Heritage Foundation, January 13, 2016. www.heritage.org.

51. Quoted in Gary Saul Morson, "Solzhenitsyn's Cathedrals," *New Criterion*, October 2017. www.newcriterion.com.

52. Doug Bandow, "Newsflash: Russia Is Not the Soviet Union," *National Interest*, December 29, 2016. http://nationalinterest.org.

53. Neil MacFarquhar, "Russian Carrier Is Bound for Syria, Flexing Muscle but Risking Malfunction," *New York Times*, October 21, 2016. www.nytimes.com.

54. Ian Buruma, "Dance with the Dragon," *New Yorker*, June 19, 2017. www.newyorker.com.

55. Quoted in This Day in Quotes, "'We Will Bury You!' (Or Something Like That)," November 18, 2016. www.thisdayinquotes.com.

56. Martin Amis, "Martin Amis on Lenin's Deadly Revolution," *New York Times*, October 16, 2017. www.nytimes.com.

For Further Research

Books

Stephen Kotkin, *Armageddon Averted: The Soviet Collapse, 1970–2000*. New York: Oxford University Press, 2008.

Andrei A. Kovalev, *Russia's Dead End: An Insider's Testimony from Gorbachev to Putin*. Lincoln, NE: Potomac, 2017.

Chris Miller, *The Struggle to Save the Soviet Economy: Mikhail Gorbachev and the Collapse of the USSR*. Chapel Hill: University of North Carolina Press, 2016.

David Remnick, *Lenin's Tomb: The Last Days of the Soviet Empire*. New York: Random House, 1994.

William Taubman, *Gorbachev: His Life and Times*. New York: Norton, 2017.

Internet Sources

Leon Aron, "Everything You Think You Know About the Collapse of the Soviet Union Is Wrong," *Foreign Policy*, June 20, 2011. http://foreignpolicy.com/2011/06/20/everything-you-think-you-know-about-the-collapse-of-the-soviet-union-is-wrong.

Rodric Braithwaite, "Fall of the Berlin Wall: The Iron Curtain Fell Because of Mikhail Gorbachev—Yet Today He Is Despised as a Traitor by Russians," *Independent* (London), November 9, 2014. www.independent.co.uk/voices/comment/fall-of-the-berlin-wall-the-iron-curtain-fell-because-of-mikhail-gorbachev-a-man-now-despised-as-a-9849117.html.

Cold War Museum, "Fall of the Soviet Union." www.coldwar.org/articles/90s/fall_of_the_soviet_union.asp.

David E. Hoffman, "How Gorbachev Slowed the Arms Race," *Washington Post*, September 21, 2009. www.washingtonpost.com/wp-dyn/content/article/2009/09/20/AR2009092002189.html.

Rameen Moshref, "The Role of Afghanistan in the Fall of the USSR," Afghanistan Online. www.afghan-web.com/history/articles/ussr.html.

National Security Archive, "Gorbachev's Nuclear Initiative of January 1986 and the Road to Reykjavik," October 12, 2016. http://nsarchive2.gwu.edu/NSAEBB/NSAEBB563-Gorbachev-nuclear-abolition-1986-and-Reykjavik-summit.

Office of the Historian, "The Collapse of the Soviet Union." https://history.state.gov/milestones/1989-1992/collapse-soviet-union.

Lewis Siegelbaum, "Perestroika and Glasnost," Seventeen Moments in Soviet History. http://soviethistory.msu.edu/1985-2/perestroika-and-glasnost.

Jonathan Steele, "10 Myths About Afghanistan," *Guardian* (Manchester), September 27, 2011. www.theguardian.com/world/2011/sep/27/10-myths-about-afghanistan.

Mark Joseph Stern, "Did Chernobyl Cause the Soviet Union to Explode?," *Slate*, January 25, 2013. www.slate.com/articles/health_and_science/nuclear_power/2013/01/chernobyl_and_the_fall_of_the_soviet_union_gorbachev_s_glasnost_allowed.html.

Websites

BBC News: Putin's Russia (www.bbc.com/news/world-europe-23357910). This BBC archive features news articles and background reports covering Vladimir Putin's years as leader of Russia after the Soviet Union's collapse.

Cold War Museum (www.coldwar.org). This site, maintained by the Cold War Museum in Warrenton, Virginia, explores the history of the Cold War by decade, from the 1940s to the 1990s. It includes many detailed articles relating to the Soviet Union's collapse.

Seventeen Moments in Soviet History (http://soviethistory.msu.edu). This site is an online archive of primary sources covering the entire history of the Soviet Union. Sources are organized by year and by topic. For example, the article "500 Days" explores the crisis of the Soviet economy during the regime's final years.

The Cold War, Alpha History (http://alphahistory.com/coldwar). This site examines various topics related to the Soviet Union and the Cold War, including détente, the Soviets in Afghanistan, Ronald Reagan, Gorbachev's reforms, and the fall of the Berlin Wall.

The Unknown Russia: Dissolving the Myths (http://russiapedia.rt.com). The Unknown Russia is a website that contains many fascinating articles about people and events in Russian history. Topics relating to the collapse of the Soviet Union include the Soviet economy, glasnost and perestroika, Boris Yeltsin, and Russia after the Soviet Union.

Index